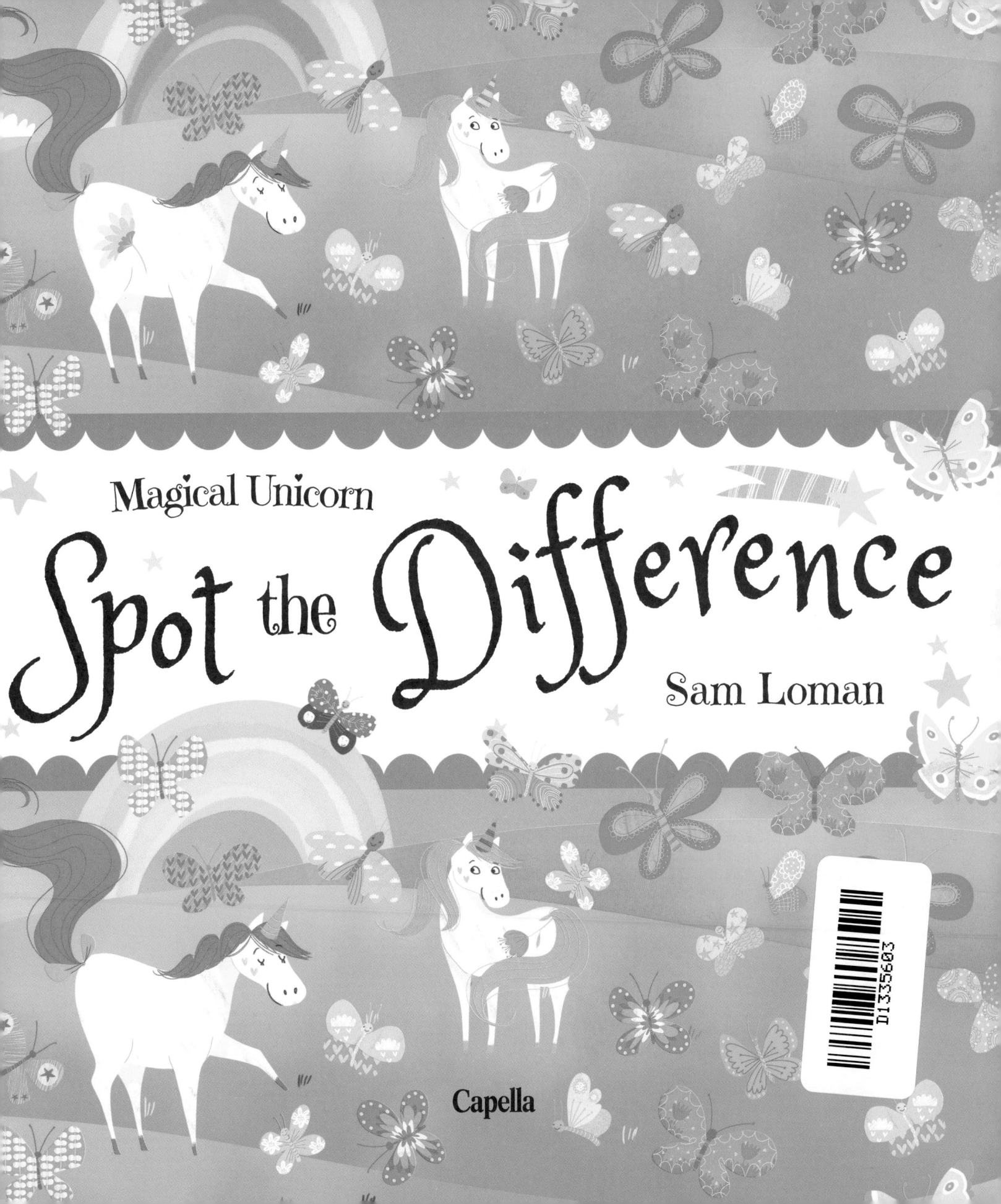

Magical Unicorn

# Spot the Difference

Sam Loman

Capella

This edition published in 2019 by Arcturus Publishing Limited
26/27 Bickels Yard, 151–153 Bermondsey Street,
London SE1 3HA, UK

Illustrated by Sam Loman
Written by Anna Brett
Edited by Susannah Bailey
Designed by Square and Circus

ISBN: 978-1-78888-892-9
CH007081NT
Supplier 33, Date 0719, Print run 9228

Printed in China

# Best Friends Forever

These two unicorns are best friends! They try to always look the same, but can you find six differences between them?

# Rainbow Magic

Unicorns can change their hair to match the stripes in a rainbow!
Spot ten differences between these two eye-catching scenes.

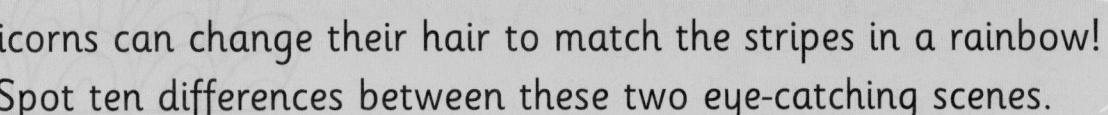

# Cupcake Count

The unicorns are setting the table for cake, but one of their yummy treats looks a bit different. Can you work out which one?

# Beautiful Butterflies

These butterflies have just hatched, and are spreading their wings for the first time. Can you spot six differences between the two scenes?

# KITTEN KISSES

Willow has come to visit her cat friend, Cloudy, and her new kittens!

They are so much fun, climbing over everything in sight.
Can you see ten differences between these two images?

# Reindeer Replacements

Santa's reindeer are sick! Luckily he's called on his unicorn friends to help pull the magic sleigh tonight.

Can you spot ten differences between the two scenes, as
Santa delivers his gifts?

# Little Ones

All the mothers have brought their babies along to the meadow to play together.
Can you see six differences between the two pictures?

# Fancy Dress

These unicorns are all dressing up as fairies for the Midsummer party!
Can you spot which one has not got her costume quite right?

# SPARKLING SEA

The unicorns are having a boat party!

**2** Describe how die cutters are used to make products from card.

................................................................................................................................

................................................................................................................................

................................................................................................................................

................................................................................................................................

................................................................................................................................ [3]

**3** Complete the table below, identifying the typical uses of the following tools with timber-based materials.

| Tool | Typical Tasks |
|---|---|
| Tenon saw | a) |
| Jack plane | b) |
| Mortise chisel | c) |
| Wood lathe | d) |
| Block plane | e) |
| CNC router | f) |

[10]

**4** Name **two** processes that can be used to make a curved product from sheets of natural timber.

1. ................................................................................................................................

2. ................................................................................................................ [2]

# Practice Questions

**5** Explain the difference between horizontal paring and vertical paring when using a chisel.

[4]

## Manufacturing Processes 3: Metals and Alloys

**6** Name two tools that cut a metal sheet by shearing.

1.

2. [2]

**7** Using notes and/or sketches, describe how a centre lathe is used to turn a metal part.

[3]

8  Describe how a product is made by die casting.

........................................................................................................................

........................................................................................................................

........................................................................................................................

........................................................................................................................

                                                                                                         [4]

# Manufacturing Processes 4: Polymers

9  **9.1)** Describe how two pieces of plastic pipe can be welded together.

........................................................................................................................

........................................................................................................................

........................................................................................................................

........................................................................................................................

........................................................................................................................

                                                                                                         [5]

**9.2)** Name an adhesive which can only be used to join polymers.

........................................................................................................................  [1]

10  Using notes and/or sketches, describe the process of press moulding polymers.

                                                                                                         [4]

# Practice Questions

## Manufacturing Processes 5: Textiles and Electronic Systems

**11** **11.1)** State two tools that can be used to cut a fabric by hand.

1. ............................................................................................................................ [1]

2. ............................................................................................................................ [1]

**11.2)** Explain the purpose of 'gathering' when making a garment from fabric.

............................................................................................................................

............................................................................................................................

............................................................................................................................

............................................................................................................................ [2]

**11.3)** Explain what is meant by 'quilting'.

............................................................................................................................

............................................................................................................................

............................................................................................................................

............................................................................................................................ [2]

**12** Describe how an electronic component is attached to a circuit board by manual soldering.

............................................................................................................................

............................................................................................................................

............................................................................................................................

............................................................................................................................

............................................................................................................................

............................................................................................................................

............................................................................................................................ [4]

# Measurement and Production Aids, and Ensuring Accuracy

**13** Explain how measurement and production aids can help to ensure accuracy when manufacturing products. Use examples to support your answer.

[12]

Total Marks ........... / 68

# Impact on Industry

**You must be able to:**

- Explain the impact of new and emerging technologies on industry and enterprise
- Discuss the potential effects of the use of new and emerging technologies on employment.

## Impact on Industry

- The use of new and emerging technologies can have an impact on the design and organisation of the workplace. This can take several forms.
  - Automation and the use of robotics:
    - **Automation** is the use of computer systems and control technology to operate equipment.
    - One example of this is the use of robots in product manufacture. This can have a very positive impact on the efficiency of manufacture.
  - The way buildings and workplaces work can be improved by new technologies. For example, self-cleaning windows keep buildings looking more aesthetically pleasing and save time and maintenance costs.
  - The increased use of computer-aided manufacture (CAM), computer numerical control (CNC) and rapid prototyping equipment means that fewer hand tools are being used in product manufacture. This allows for greater accuracy and consistency of manufacture.

> ### Key Point
>
> Automation in manufacture can help to increase the efficiency of production.

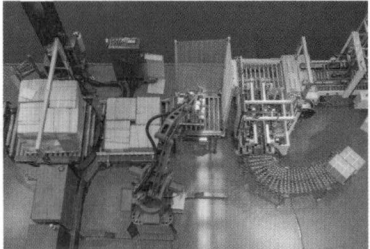

Robotic arm being used in product manufacture

## Impact on Enterprise

- Effective business innovation helps to drive enterprise. This can take many different forms.

### Crowd Funding

- **Crowd funding** is a way for people to raise awareness and money for a project or idea. The enterprise will typically have a funding 'goal' that needs to be met.
- People donate money in return for rewards.
- The internet has made crowd funding very easy to implement. Websites can be set up with online payment options for people to use. Providers of crowd-funding websites typically take a percentage of the money raised.
- Crowd funding is useful for independent people or 'start-up' businesses who might struggle to gain access to more conventional sources of funding.

The use of social media to promote products is a key part of virtual marketing and retail

### Virtual Marketing and Retail

- Virtual marketing is the use of web-based marketing techniques.
- This includes the use of website banner advertising, email marketing and social media to promote products.

### Co-operatives

- A co-operative is a business or organisation that is run jointly by its members.
- The members share in the benefits or profits that are made.
- A co-operative benefits from the buying power of its entire membership and its democratic structure.
- A small number of people can form a co-operative, making them easy to set up.

### Fair Trade

- Fair trade is a movement that works to help people in developing countries get a fair deal for the products that they produce (for more information on fair trade see page 17).

### Planned Obsolescence

- Planned obsolescence is a business strategy where a product is designed to be no longer useful after a set period of time. This could be in terms of function, compatibility or how fashionable it is. This often results in a new or improved product replacing it.

## Impact on Employment

- One major consideration regarding the use of new and emerging technologies is the potential effect on employment.
- Many are concerned that, for example, increased automation in the workplace will result in fewer jobs being available.
- The increase in the use of CAD/CAM has resulted in fewer jobs for skilled hand machine workers, but more jobs for people trained in the use and maintenance of CAM equipment.
- Companies need to have the capacity to retrain their staff to be able to make effective use of new and emerging technologies in the workplace. In addition, workers themselves need to be increasingly flexible and able to update their skills in response to change.
- Technological change will always result in changes to job roles, particularly in design and technology. Many important jobs didn't exist as little as 5–10 years ago, and this trend is likely to grow. For example, mobile apps did not exist prior to the development of the smartphone, let alone app designers.
- Workers in the modern design and technology workplace must be literate in the use of computer-based tools.

> **Key Point**
>
> Co-operatives are run by and for the benefit of their members.

The increased use of automation has resulted in changes to the job roles of people

> **Quick Test**
>
> 1. What is crowd funding?
> 2. What is a co-operative?
> 3. What are the potential impacts of automation on employment?

> **Key Words**
>
> automation
> crowd funding
> co-operative

# Impact on Production

**You must be able to:**

- Explain the impact of CAD and CAM on production
- Explain how production techniques and systems improve manufacturing efficiency.

## CAD

- **CAD** stands for **computer-aided design**.
- It is the use of computer software to produce designs for products. The designs can be 2D drawings or 3D models.

A designer using CAD software

### Advantages of CAD

- CAD is extremely accurate, often more accurate than drawing designs by hand.
- It is easier to modify or revise an existing design.
- Storage space is reduced.
- Files can be shared around the world very quickly, or imported into presentations.
- 3D models can be rotated and viewed from different angles.
- Designs can be simulated to see how well they will function. This allows potential problems to be spotted early.
- Designs can be exported to CAM equipment for manufacture.

### Disadvantages of CAD

- Some CAD packages are expensive to buy, so there can be high initial setup costs.
- There needs to be access to appropriate ICT hardware to run the software. This usually needs to be a computer with a very good specification, which adds to the cost.
- Some designers may not be familiar with how to use CAD software, so time and money must be spent training them. They must also regularly update their skills.

## CAM

- **CAM** stands for **computer-aided manufacture**.
- It is the use of computer software to control machine tools to manufacture products.
- Examples of CAM equipment include laser cutters, vinyl cutters and 3D plotters.

### Key Point

CAD/CAM improve accuracy of design and manufacture, but often require high initial setup costs to be paid.

### Advantages of CAM

- Complex shapes can be produced much more easily than when manufacturing by hand.
- There is consistency of manufacture as every product produced is exactly the same.
- It enables very high levels of manufacturing precision and accuracy.
- There is greater efficiency as machines can run 24 hours a day, 7 days a week.
- It can increase the speed of manufacture, especially when producing products in large numbers.

**Disadvantages of CAM**

- As with CAD initial setup costs can be high. CAM machines are usually very expensive, although their cost is reducing with time.
- Operators must be trained to use the equipment, which adds time and cost.
- For one-off products, CAM can actually be slower than if the product was produced by hand.

# Improving Manufacturing Efficiency

- **Lean manufacturing** is an approach that aims to make products in the most effective and efficient way possible. Lean manufacturing involves eliminating all forms of waste during manufacturing. Waste here is not referring just to rubbish or removed material: it refers to any activity that does not add value to the product. For example, waste includes:
    - moving products around a factory
    - time workers spend looking for tools
    - making too many products
    - doing more to the product than the customer needs
    - making defective parts.
- Typically, most manufacturers have a stock of materials waiting to be processed. This is a waste as stock costs money, which is tied up in the company. With **just-in-time production** (JIT production), suppliers deliver materials only when they are needed. This means less money is tied up in materials. However, if suppliers don't deliver on time or there are quality problems, this can stop production, meaning that expensive equipment is standing around unused and deadlines are missed.
- Flexible manufacturing systems (FMS) can react in the event of predicted or unpredicted change. This can include the need for the system to be changed to make new products or changes to the order of operations that make a product.
- Increased automation is improving manufacturing efficiency, but can result in fewer jobs for people.

# Technology Push and Market Pull

- **Technology push** is when new products are produced because of new materials or manufacturing methods becoming available. Research and development is a key part of this process.
- **Market pull** is when new products are developed because of market forces. Market research is a common tool used by design companies to gauge the opinion of the marketplace.

A laser cutter in operation

> **Key Point**
>
> Different production systems and techniques can be used to improve manufacturing efficiency.

Automation can be used to improve manufacturing efficiency

> **Key Words**
>
> computer-aided design (CAD)
> computer-aided manufacture (CAM)
> lean manufacturing
> just-in-time production
> technology push
> market pull

> **Quick Test**
>
> 1. What is meant by the terms 'CAD' and 'CAM'?
> 2. What is lean manufacturing?
> 3. What is the difference between technology push and market pull?

# Impact on Society and the Environment

**You must be able to:**

- Explain the impact of new and emerging technologies on sustainability and the environment
- Discuss the potential effects of new designs on culture and society.

## Impact on Sustainability and the Environment

- Resource consumption, such as the sourcing of raw materials, impacts on the future of the planet.
- Finite resources are resources that will eventually run out. For example, many products are made using timber-based products. Trees should be replanted to ensure a continuous supply and prevent deforestation.
- Non-finite resources are resources that are easy to replenish. Making greater use of these can help to improve the sustainability of products.
- Designers should aim to reduce the amount of waste that is created through designing, making and using products. This can be achieved by making products from recyclable or biodegradable materials, or making products easy to disassemble or reuse.
- New and emerging technologies can have an impact on the environment. This can be done in numerous ways:
  - **Continuous improvement** is where ongoing incremental improvements are made to a product or process.
  - Efficient working can reduce waste, in terms of both time and resources.
  - Pollution is a major contributor to global warming. New technologies can help to reduce this. For example, electric cars are starting to replace vehicles with pollution-causing petrol engines.

A tree being planted to replace one that has been cut down

### Key Point

New technologies can be used to reduce pollution, such as electric car engines.

## Impact on Culture

- Changes in fashion and **trends** can be affected and influenced by new and emergent technologies.
  - Product designs are often influenced by what is 'in fashion' at the time. For example, clothing designs.
  - This can change continuously and designers need to keep on top of current trends if they are to keep on producing popular products.

### Key Point

Trends can be started through the emergence and subsequent use of new technologies.

- New technologies can create trends. For example, Apple's use of applications, or apps, in their iPhone completely changed how people used their mobile phones. Apps came from nowhere to becoming something that users 'must have' on their phone.
- People with different faiths and beliefs should be respected when designing new products.

## Impact on Society

- Products can also have effects on wider society. These can be both positive and negative. Sometimes these effects are unexpected or unintended.
    - For example, mobile smartphones have completely changed how people communicate with each other in the last decade.
    - Although this means it is easier than ever to communicate with people in different locations, some feel a negative impact on society is that people do not talk directly with each other as much.
- Products should be developed so that they do not have a negative impact on others.
    - Disabled people have specific needs that must be catered for. For example, cash machines are positioned lower on walls so they can be accessed by people in wheelchairs.
    - The elderly also have specific needs and products can be designed to support them. For example, a mobile phone designed with large buttons and text.
    - Designers must also be careful not to offend people from different religious backgrounds. An example of where this can go wrong is the plastic UK £5 note that was introduced in 2016. This was found to contain animal fat, which was a problem for some Hindus and Sikhs, many of whom are vegetarian.

Apps on an Apple iPhone

### Inclusive and Exclusive Design

- **Inclusive design** is about designing products and systems that can be used by everyone. Ideally this should be without any special adaptations.
- Exclusive design is when products are designed for a particular group of people or a limited audience. For example, car seats are designed specifically for babies or very young children.

A mobile phone designed with large buttons and text for elderly people

---

### Quick Test

1. What is the difference between finite and non-finite resources?
2. How can designers reduce waste when designing and making new products?
3. Why do designers need to consider people with different religious beliefs?

### Key Words

continuous improvement
trend
inclusive design

# Review Questions

## Scales of Manufacture, and Manufacturing Processes 1 and 2

**1**   **1.1)**   State what is meant by batch manufacturing.

[2]

**1.2)**   Give **three** examples of products that are made by batch manufacturing.

1.

2.

3.    [3]

**2**   Using notes and/or sketches, describe how the offset lithography process is carried out.

[5]

**3** The picture shows a drill.

Identify **three** safety precautions that should be taken when using the drill. For each, give a reason why it is needed.

Bench drill

| Safety Precaution | Reason this is Needed |
|---|---|
| **1.** | |
| **2.** | |
| **3.** | |

[6]

**4** Describe how a curved shape is made in natural timber by steam bending.

[5]

# Review Questions

## Manufacturing Processes 3: Metals and Alloys

**5** Name **two** methods that can be used to bend a metal sheet.

1. .............................................................................................................................................

2. ............................................................................................................................................. [2]

**6** Complete the table, identifying the tools or machines that would be used to carry out the task listed.

| Task | Tool or Machine Typically Used |
|---|---|
| Cutting a metal bar by hand | a) |
| Turning a circular profile on a metal bar | b) |
| Making a hole in a metal plate | c) |
| Making a flat or a groove in a metal part | d) |

[4]

**7** A manufacturer has an order from a customer for 10 identical cast parts.

Explain why the manufacturer might prefer to use sand casting rather than die casting for this task.

.............................................................................................................................................

.............................................................................................................................................

.............................................................................................................................................

.............................................................................................................................................

.............................................................................................................................................

.............................................................................................................................................

.............................................................................................................................................

.............................................................................................................................................

............................................................................................................................................. [4]

# Manufacturing Processes 4: Polymers

**8** Name **two** types of saw that are used to cut polymer sheet.

1. ...........................................................................................................................................................

2. ........................................................................................................................................................... [2]

**9** Explain how a polymer part is produced by 3D printing.

.................................................................................................................................................................

.................................................................................................................................................................

.................................................................................................................................................................

.................................................................................................................................................................

.................................................................................................................................................................

................................................................................................................................................................. [4]

**10** Using notes and/or sketches, describe how a plastic bottle is made by blow moulding.

[4]

# Review Questions

## Manufacturing Processes 5: Textiles and Electronic Systems

**11** State what an overlocker is used for in textiles.

[1]

**12** Describe how rotary screen printing is used in textile manufacturing.

[4]

**13** Explain the differences between manual and flow soldering.

[6]

# Measurement and Production Aids, and Ensuring Accuracy

**14** **14.1)** Define the following terms.

Jig

.................................................................................................................................

.................................................................................................................................

.................................................................................................................................

Tolerance

.................................................................................................................................

.................................................................................................................................

.................................................................................................................................  [4]

**14.2)** Explain why it is important to use tolerances when manufacturing products.

.................................................................................................................................

.................................................................................................................................

.................................................................................................................................

.................................................................................................................................

.................................................................................................................................

.................................................................................................................................  [3]

Total Marks .................... / 59

# Practice Questions

## Impact on Industry, and Impact on Society and Environment

**1**

**1.1)** Which of the following statements best describes the term 'co-operative'?
Tick the correct box.

**a)** A business jointly owned and run by its members. ☐

**b)** A method of marketing and selling a product. ☐

**c)** A method of raising funding and awareness for a project. ☐

**d)** A way of ensuring producers of products get a fair deal. ☐ [1]

**1.2)** Explain why it is important to consider people of different cultures when designing products. Include an example in your answer.

_____

_____

_____

_____

_____

[3]

**1.3)** Explain **one** benefit of using continuous improvement techniques in manufacturing.

_____

_____

_____

[2]

# Impact on Production

**2** Give **three** advantages and **two** disadvantages of using CAD to design prototypes.

Advantage 1

Advantage 2

Advantage 3

Disadvantage 1

Disadvantage 2

[5]

Total Marks _____ / 11

# Review Questions

## Impact on Industry, and Impact on Society and Environment

**1**   **1.1)**   Give **two** advantages and **one** disadvantage of increased automation in manufacturing.

Advantage 1

.......................................................................................................................................................

.......................................................................................................................................................

Advantage 2

.......................................................................................................................................................

.......................................................................................................................................................

Disadvantage

.......................................................................................................................................................

....................................................................................................................................... [3]

**1.2)**   Describe the difference between a finite and a non-finite resource.

.......................................................................................................................................................

.......................................................................................................................................................

.......................................................................................................................................................

....................................................................................................................................... [2]

## Impact on Production

**2** Give **three** advantages and **two** disadvantages of using CAM to produce prototypes.

Advantage 1

..................................................................................................................................................................

..................................................................................................................................................................

Advantage 2

..................................................................................................................................................................

..................................................................................................................................................................

Advantage 3

..................................................................................................................................................................

..................................................................................................................................................................

Disadvantage 1

..................................................................................................................................................................

..................................................................................................................................................................

Disadvantage 2

..................................................................................................................................................................

..................................................................................................................................................................

[5]

Total Marks .................... / 10

# Mixed Exam-Style Questions

1  A manufacturer is making a plastic product using the injection moulding process.

**1.1)** Using notes and/or sketches, describe the injection moulding process.

[5]

**1.2)** The volume of plastic in one product is $2.4 \times 10^{-5}$ m³. After making 20 000 products, the manufacturer finds that he has used 0.5 m³ of material.

Calculate the volume of material that has been lost as waste during the manufacturing process.

[2]

**1.3)** The manufacturer has calculated that the total cost of each product will be £6.40.

The selling price is £8.00. Calculate the percentage profit.

[2]

2  Using notes and/or sketches, describe how a product is made using sand casting.

[10]

# Mixed Exam-Style Questions

**3** The table lists the tools and equipment used for wasting different materials.

Complete the missing information. The first row has been completed as an example.

| Material | Tool | Used for |
|---|---|---|
| Paper | Punch | Making holes |
| Wood | a) | Making straight cuts by hand |
| Thin card | Compass cutters | b) |
| c) | Metal shears | Cutting thin sheet |
| d) | Rotary trimmer | e) |
| Textiles | f) | Cutting a serrated edge to stop material fraying |
| Metal | g) | Turning round parts |

[7]

4    A design is being produced for a child's night light. The night light must:

- Automatically detect when it has become dark

- Light up for a timed period after it has gone dark.

**4.1)**   Give a suitable input and output device for the night light.

Input

................................................................................................................................................

Output

................................................................................................................................................ [2]

**4.2)**   The designer has decided to use a microcontroller as the process of the system.

Explain **two** reasons why this would be a good choice.

**1.** ...........................................................................................................................................

................................................................................................................................................

................................................................................................................................................

................................................................................................................................................

**2.** ...........................................................................................................................................

................................................................................................................................................

................................................................................................................................................

................................................................................................................................................ [4]

# Mixed Exam-Style Questions

**5** Complete the table, which lists how mechanical devices convert between types of motion. The first line has been completed as an example.

| Device | Type of Motion Input | Type of Motion Output |
|---|---|---|
| Pulley | Rotary motion | Rotary motion |
| a) | Linear motion | Linear motion in opposite direction |
| Rack and pinion | b) | c) |
| Cam | Rotary | d) |

[4]

**6** A team of designers is developing an electric vehicle. To transfer the motion from the motor to the wheels they are considering using either pulleys and belts or two spur gears. Compare the advantages and disadvantages of these two approaches.

...........................................................................................................................................

...........................................................................................................................................

...........................................................................................................................................

...........................................................................................................................................

...........................................................................................................................................

...........................................................................................................................................

...........................................................................................................................................

...........................................................................................................................................

...........................................................................................................................................

........................................................................................................................................... [6]

**7**   **7.1)** Explain how designers can ensure that their products are sustainable.

_____

_____

_____

_____

_____

_____

_____

[4]

**7.2)** Define the term 'product miles'.

_____

_____

_____

[2]

**7.3)** Explain why it is important to reduce oceanic pollution.

_____

_____

_____

[2]

**8** Identify the types of motion represented by each of the diagrams.

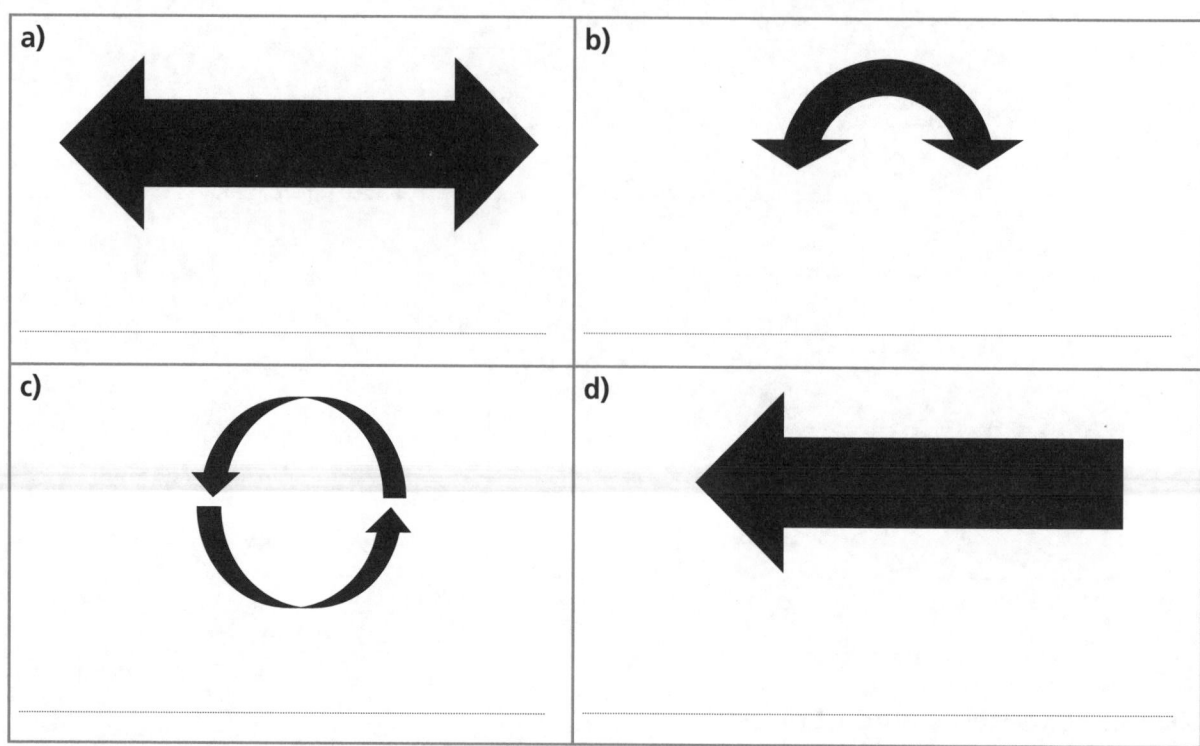

a)

b)

c)

d)

[4]

**9** The diagram shows a lever.

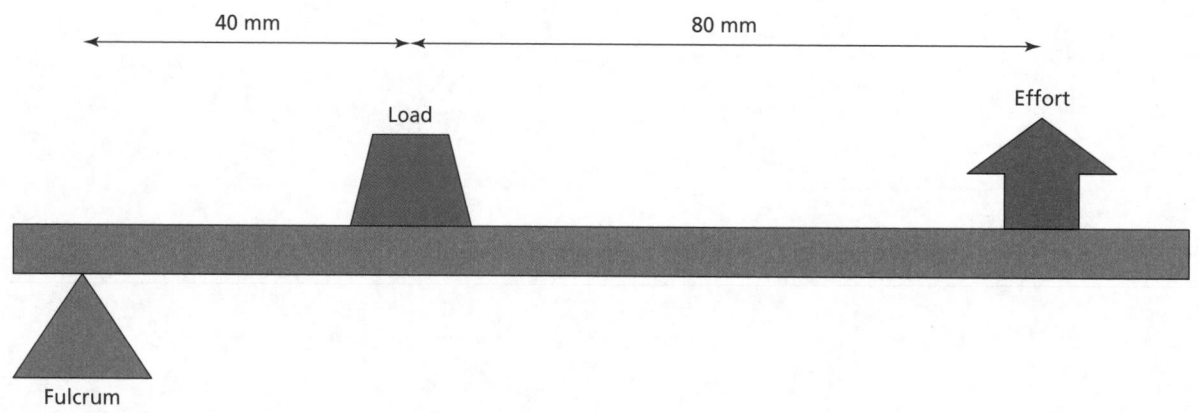

40 mm    80 mm

Load

Effort

Fulcrum

**9.1)** State the order of the lever.

[1]

**9.2)** The load is 40 mm from the fulcrum. The effort is 80 mm from the load.

Calculate the mechanical advantage.

[2]

**10** **10.1)** State what is meant by just-in-time manufacturing.

[1]

**10.2)** Why do companies use just-in-time manufacturing?

[3]

# Mixed Exam-Style Questions

**11** Using notes and/or sketches, describe how extruded tubes are made from polymer.

[5]

**12** Identify **two** computer-based tools that are used in the design and communication of products. For each, explain how it is used.

Computer-based tool 1

Explanation

[3]

Computer-based tool 2

Explanation

[3]

**13** **13.1)** Explain **two** advantages and **one** disadvantage of just-in-time manufacturing.

Advantage 1 ...............................................................................................................................

.............................................................................................................................................

.............................................................................................................................................

.............................................................................................................................................

Advantage 2 ...............................................................................................................................

.............................................................................................................................................

.............................................................................................................................................

.............................................................................................................................................

Disadvantage ............................................................................................................................

.............................................................................................................................................

.............................................................................................................................................

............................................................................................................................................. **[6]**

**13.2)** Explain the purpose of lean manufacturing.

.............................................................................................................................................

.............................................................................................................................................

.............................................................................................................................................

............................................................................................................................................. **[2]**

**Total Marks** ................ / 80

# Answers

**Page 9 Quick Test**
1. A cyclic design approach where each iteration is tested, evaluated and refined, resulting in a new iteration.
2. Greater sense of user ownership in final product; constant user feedback.
3. When designing electronic, mechanical or mechatronic systems.

**Page 11 Quick Test**
1. Input, process, driver and output
2. They have a resistance that varies depending on the light level.
3. Flowcharts, block editors or raw code
4. Light: lamp; sound, buzzer or speaker

**Page 13 Quick Test**
1. Norman Foster/Foster + Partners
2. Bauhaus
3. Aldo Rossi.
4. Sir Alec Issigonis

**Page 15 Quick Test**
1. It combined computing/internet technology with a digital music player and a mobile phone.
2. The bagless vacuum cleaner
3. To keep athletes cool and dry
4. To eliminate harmful toxins from its clothing

**Page 17 Quick Test**
1. Reduce, rethink, refuse, recycle, reuse, repair
2. Guaranteed minimum price for most products; Fairtrade Premium to spend on improving lifestyles
3. Damage to marine life and habitats

**Design Strategies and Electronic Systems**
1. **1.1)** 1 mark for each correct response.

| Function | Component | Input, Process or Output |
|---|---|---|
| Detect changes in light level | LDR [1] | Input [1] |
| Produce light | Lamp [1] | Output [1] |
| Produce sound | Buzzer [1] or speaker [1] | Output [1] |
| Detect changes in temperature | Thermistor [1] | Input [1] |
| Be programmed to turn an output on for a set period of time | Microcontroller [1] | Process [1] |

   **1.2)** 1 mark for definition. For example: a framework where the needs and wants of users are given attention at each stage of the design process [1].

   **The Work of Others: Designers**
2. 1 mark for each designer, 1 mark for each appropriate design and up to 2 marks for each explanation of influence. For example:
   * Designer: Harry Beck [1]; design: London Underground Map [1]; influence: used a layout inspired by electronic schematics [1] which has been emulated for use in many transport systems worldwide [1].
   * Designer: Norman Foster [1]; design: 30 St Mary Axe/the 'Gherkin' [1]; influence: pioneered energy-saving methods [1] which allowed it to use half the energy of similar sized buildings [1].

**The Work of Others: Companies**
3. 1 mark for each company, 1 mark for each appropriate design and up to 2 marks for each explanation of influence. For example:
   * Company: Alessi [1]; design: Juicy Salif lemon squeezer [1]; influence: has a distinctive form [1], showing that everyday household objects can be designed to be interesting to look at [1].
   * Company: Apple [1]; design: iPhone [1]; influence: reinvented the concept of the mobile phone [1] by combining a phone with a digital music player and internet capability [1].

**Ecological, Environmental and Social Issues**
4. For each term award 1 mark for correct definition. Reuse: using the materials/components again in another product [1]. Recycle: reprocessing the materials/components used for use in another product [1]. Refuse: deciding not to use unsustainable materials/components in a product [1]. Rethink: finding a better, more sustainable way to solve the design problem [1]. Reduce: using less material/fewer components in the product [1]. Repair: designing the product so it is easy to fix if it breaks [1].

**Page 23 Quick Test**
1. A group of people assembled to discuss and give feedback on a product or a product idea.
2. Primary data is from original research, secondary data is from other sources.
3. Measurements taken from millions of people and put in charts. Used to ensure products are easy to use and interact with.

**Page 25 Quick Test**
1. A short description of the design problem and how it is to be solved.
2. A set of measurable criteria for the design.
3. Details surrounding scale of production, assembly details, materials needed and quality control and quality assurance.

**Page 27 Quick Test**
1. Sketching, modelling, testing, evaluation
2. To get first ideas down on paper quickly.
3. To check the effectiveness of a pattern that has been produced for a garment.
4. It uses real components, so is accurate.

**Page 29 Quick Test**
1. Freehand, perspective, isometric projection
2. 30°
3. To show how the parts in an assembly fit together.

**Page 31 Quick Test**
1. Plan/top, front and side
2. For example, any two of: calculating the values of components to use in an electrical circuit, designing the shape of speedboat hulls, determining how strong a bridge needs to be, simulating the testing of products.
3. Card modelling, toiles, breadboarding

**Page 33 Quick Test**
1. Allows face-to-face meetings to take place from different locations, almost anywhere in the world.
2. Produces visual aids that add interest to a presentation; allows sharing of photographs and technical information of a design.
3. Bill of materials

**Page 35 Quick Test**
1. A full-sized, actual version or primary example of an intended product or system.
2. So the designer can ensure that the final product meets their needs.
3. So the designer can learn how well the product being developed would meet the needs of the brief, specification and/or client.

**Design Strategies, and Ecological, Environmental and Social Issues**
1. 1.1) Up to 2 marks for explanation of one benefit. For example: guarantees a minimum price for most products [1] so that even if global prices fall producers will still get a fair price [1].
   1.2) Up to 2 marks for explanation. For example: it might cost more to buy [1] which would make it unappealing for people on tight budgets [1].
   1.3) 1 mark for definition of the term. For example: the clearing of forest area into non-forest land [1].
   1.4) Up to 2 marks for explanation. For example: a cyclic process where each iteration of a design is tested and evaluated [1]. Changes and refinements are then made, leading to a new iteration [1].

**Electronic Systems**
2. 1 mark for showing how/where the program starts and ends, 1 mark for way of checking the switch has been pressed, 1 mark for turning on the buzzer after the switch has been pressed, 1 mark for way of setting the correct time period, 1 mark for turning the buzzer off, 1 mark for turning on the lamp. Any appropriate programming language may be used, including raw code, block or flowchart-based approaches.

**The Work of Others: Designers**
3. 1 mark for each designer and up to 3 marks for each description of impact. For example:
   - Designer: Mary Quant [1]; impact: was an influential figure in the popular Mod fashion movement [1]. Encouraged people to dress to please themselves [1]. Took credit for the design of the miniskirt [1].
   - Designer: Gerrit Rietveld [1]; impact: part of the De Stijl design movement [1]. Designed famous red and blue chair [1]. Aimed for simplicity in construction [1].

**The Work of Others: Companies**
4. 1 mark for each company, 1 mark for each product and up to 2 marks for each description. For example:
   - Company: Dyson [1]; product: bagless vacuum cleaner [1]; description; uses cyclone to separate dust [1], stores dirt in see through plastic container [1].
   - Company: Under Armour [1]; product: moisture-wicking t-shirt [1]; description: made from moisture-wicking synthetic fabric [1], keeps athletes cool and dry [1].

**Research and Investigation**
1. 1.1) Up to 2 marks. For example: measurements taken from large numbers of people [1] and put together in charts [1].
   1.2) Up to 3 marks for explanation. For example: check charts showing head circumferences [1]. This would assist in creating appropriate sizes for the helmet design [1] so that it would properly fit a large number of firefighters [1].
   1.3) 1 mark for each correct definition. Primary data: data that is obtained first hand [1]. Secondary data: data that is available/obtained from other parties [1].

**Briefs and Specifications**
2. 1 mark for each correct answer. 2.1) d;   2.2) c;   2.3) b

**Exploring and Developing Ideas**
3. 3.1) 1 mark for each appropriate answer. For example: Electronic circuit: breadboard [1]; wedding dress: toile [1]; early idea for a mobile phone case: card model [1].
   3.2) 1 mark for each correct answer. For example: sketching [1], testing [1], evaluating [1].

**Communication of Ideas**
4. Award marks as follows, up to a maximum of 4 marks:
   - Correctly identifying/using the vanishing point, extended from the wall edges [1].

- Vertical lines are all at 90° to the horizontal plane/horizon line [1].
- Horizontal lines in cooker extend towards the vanishing point [1].
- Cooker is correctly located half way along the right wall [1].
- Cooker is well drawn and in appropriate size [1].

5. Award 1 mark each for up to three of the following, with a second mark for each for stating its use:
   - 3D CAD drawing [1], for example to show how parts in an assembly fit together [1].
   - Card modelling [1] or 3D printing [1], for example to create the physical appearance of the item [1].
   - Producing a toile [1] to test the design for a garment [1].
   - Breadboarding [1] to test the operation of a circuit [1].

**Computer-Based Tools**
6. 1 mark for each suitable example and 1 mark each for further description.
   - Produce a bill of materials to show the client [1] using spreadsheet software [1].
   - Produce a visual presentation of initial design ideas [1] using presentation software [1].
   - Produce a simulation of how the design works [1] using CAD software [1].

**Prototype Development**
7. 7.1) 1 mark per suitable point or 2 marks for a point explained further. For example: shows how the product will look/function [1] so that clients can decide if they are happy or not with the design [1]. Potential problems with the design can be identified early [1] thus ensuring the final product is fit for purpose [1].
   7.2) 1 mark per suitable point or 2 marks for a point explained further. For example: it is easy to cut to size/shape [1] so specialist cutting tools are not needed [1]. It is cheap to buy [1] so can be used in large quantities [1].

**Page 47 Quick Test**
1. They are burned to create steam. This then turns turbines, which drive the generators that produce electricity.
2. Solar, wind, hydro-electrical, tidal and biomass
3. They are clean, sustainable and will not run out.

**Page 49 Quick Test**
1. Both move back and forwards, but reciprocating motion is in a straight line whereas oscillating motion swings down and up.
2. Rigid bar, fulcrum, load and effort
3. Third-order lever

**Page 51 Quick Test**
1. Rotary to reciprocating motion
2. Spur, bevel, worm and worm wheel, rack and pinion
3. It would make the pulley wheels run in opposite directions.

**Research and Investigation**
1. 1 mark for each correct answer. 1.1) d; 1.2) c; 1.3) a

**Briefs and Specifications**
2. Up to 2 marks for each definition. Design brief: a short description of the design problem [1] and how it is to be solved [1]. Design specification: a set of measurable design targets [1] that the product must meet [1]. Manufacturing specification: a set of information about how the product is to be manufactured [1] such as scale of production [1].

**Exploring and Developing Ideas**
3. 7–9 marks: thorough knowledge and understanding of the steps taken when developing design ideas using an iterative

# Answers

process. All points fully explained. 4–6 marks: good knowledge and understanding of the importance of the steps taken when developing design ideas using an iterative process. Some points explained further. 1–3 marks: limited knowledge or understanding. Mainly descriptive response.

Indicative answer: iterative process: a cyclic process where each iteration is tested, evaluated and refined, leading to a new iteration. Sketching: a quick way to get initial ideas down on paper; freehand sketching does not need to follow drawing conventions. Modelling: models are made to check how a design will look and function in 3D. They can also be presented to clients and stakeholders to gain feedback. Card is a good modelling material to use as it is cheap and easy to cut. Testing and evaluating: each iteration of a design should be tested and evaluated to assess how well it does the job that it is supposed to do. The client or end user should be involved in this process. This then leads to refinements and improvements being made.

### Communication of Ideas

4. To show how the parts of a product are located in relation to each other [1]. It can be used when assembling products [1].
5. Award up to two marks as follows: 'horizontal' lines are positioned at 30° to the baseline [1]; vertical lines (such as the front edge) go straight up [1]; lines are in proportion to the size of the object [1].
6. 6.1) Third angle [1]
   6.2) i) Top/plan [1]
        ii) Front [1]
        iii) Side [1]

### Computer-Based Tools

7. 1 mark for each correct answer. 7.1) d; 7.2) a; 7.3) b

### Prototype Development

8. 7–9 marks: thorough knowledge and understanding of the considerations that designers must take account of when developing prototypes. All points fully discussed. 4–6 marks: good knowledge and understanding of the considerations that designers must take account of when developing prototypes. Some points discussed further. 1–3 marks: limited knowledge or understanding. Mainly descriptive response.

Indicative answer: does it satisfy the requirements of the brief, the specification and the client? Has the client been consulted or given feedback on the prototype? Is the prototype innovative or creative? Will it offer something original to the market? Does it function as expected? Is it fit for its intended purpose? Is it aesthetically pleasing? How does it appeal to the five senses? Is it easily marketable? Will it fill a gap in the market?

## Pages 58–59 Practice Questions

### Energy Generation and Storage

1. 1.1) 1 mark for each specific non-renewable source, such as coal, oil, gas or nuclear.
   1.2) 1 mark for each specific renewable source other than wind, such as solar, biomass or hydro-electricity.
   1.3) Up to 2 marks for explanation of advantage and 2 marks for explanation of disadvantage. For example:
   - Advantage: better for the environment than using fossil fuels [1] as it does not release harmful greenhouse gases into the atmosphere [1].
   - Disadvantage: will not generate electricity when there is no wind [1] which means it is limited for use on products that will be placed in windy areas [1].

### Mechanical Systems

2. 2.1) Movement in a straight line in one direction [1].
   2.2) Movement in a circle [1].

2.3) Movement backwards and forwards [1].
2.4) Swinging backwards and forwards [1].
3. 3.1) Anticlockwise [1]
   3.2) Gear ratio = 12 / 36 [1 mark for method] = 1 : 3 [1 mark for answer; must be a ratio, fractions not accepted]

## Pages 60–81 Revise Questions

### Page 61 Quick Test

1. Tension, compression, torsion, shear, bending
2. Density, thermal conductivity, electrical conductivity
3. Elasticity means that a material will return to its original shape, whereas ductility is the amount of permanent change in shape.

### Page 63 Quick Test

1. Bleached card
2. Grams per square metre, which indicates the thickness of paper or card.
3. Recycled paper cannot be used in products for food packaging.

### Page 65 Quick Test

1. Oak, birch, ash, mahogany, balsa
2. Pine, larch, spruce
3. MDF, plywood, chipboard

### Page 67 Quick Test

1. A mixture of two or more metals
2. Any three of: stainless steel, brass, high-speed steel
3. Hard and brittle, but becomes malleable between 100 and 150°C

### Page 69 Quick Test

1. Carbon-based fossil fuels
2. Liquid resins and powders
3. For example ropes, carpets, packaging

### Page 71 Quick Test

1. Knitted, woven, non-woven
2. Cotton, wool, silk
3. Coal and oil

### Page 73 Quick Test

1. Carbon
2. Less than 100 nanometres
3. Glass-reinforced polyester (GRP), carbon-reinforced polyester (CRP)

### Page 75 Quick Test

1. Nuts and bolts, rivets, machine screws (also accept hinges)
2. Screw
3. Gears, cams, pulleys, belts

### Page 77 Quick Test

1. To improve function or aesthetics
2. Polishing
3. A tactile effect and improved visual look of the product
4. To reduce the effects of friction, such as heat and noise

### Page 79 Quick Test

1. Functionality (mechanical and physical properties), aesthetics, cost, availability, environmental, social, cultural, ethical
2. Surface finish, texture, colour
3. Electrical conductivity (insulator), toughness

### Page 81 Quick Test

1. To increase the malleability
2. Folding, bending, laminating
3. Ribs of material, normally located on the inside of a product, which increase the stiffness

# Answers

**Energy Generation and Storage**

1. 1.1) Up to 2 marks for explanation of each advantage. For example:
   - They are more sustainable [1] as less battery waste needs to be thrown away [1].
   - They can be recharged hundreds of times [1] so save on cost of buying new batteries [1].
   1.2) Up to 2 marks for explanation of an advantage and 2 marks for explanation of a disadvantage. For example:
   - Advantage: it can be better for the environment [1] as it is carbon-neutral [1].
   - Disadvantage: it involves the growing and caring for of crops [1] which makes it an expensive way of producing fuel [1].

**Mechanical Systems**

2. 2.1) 1 mark for a suitable example; for example, scissors, pliers, seesaw.
   2.2) Effort = load / mechanical advantage [1] = 24 / 3 = 8 Newtons [1]
   2.3) The effort needed for movement is greater than the load [1], because the effort is nearer the fulcrum than the load [1].
3. 3.1) Push–pull linkage [1]
   3.2) Bevel gears or worm and worm wheel [1]
   3.3) Cam [1]
   3.4) Rack and pinion [1]

**Properties of Materials**

1. 1.1) The ability to withstand a pulling force [1].
   1.2) The mass of material per unit volume [1].

**Materials: Paper and Board**

2. Award up to 6 marks as follows (information can be in either sketches or notes): trees are cut down [1] and turned into pulp [1]. Chemicals are added [1], such as chalk and dye [1], and the paper is formed using a mesh [1]. It is then wound into rolls [1] and subsequently cut to the required size [1].

**Materials: Timber**

3. 3.1).i) 1 mark for an appropriate answer, for example pine, larch, spruce [1].
   ii) 1 mark for a typical application of that softwood. For example (pine) construction work, joinery, furniture, (larch) boats and yachts, exterior cladding of buildings, interior panelling, (spruce) general construction, wooden aircraft frames.
   iii) 1 mark each for identifying a requirement of the application and justifying the choice with respect to one of the material properties (for example strength, weight, resistance to decay, aesthetics).
   3.2) i) 1 mark for an appropriate answer, for example oak, birch, ash, mahogany, balsa [1].
   ii) 1 mark for a typical application of that hardwood. For example (oak) high-quality furniture, (birch) furniture and cabinets, turned items, (ash) tool handles, sports equipment, wooden ladders, (mahogany) high-quality furniture, (balsa) modelling.
   iii) 1 mark each for identifying a requirement of the application and justifying the choice with respect to one of the material properties (for example strength, weight, ability to be worked, resistance to moisture, aesthetics).
4. 1 mark each for any two of: rough sawn planks, PSE planks, mouldings.

**Materials: Metals**

5. Award up to 4 marks as follows (information can be in either sketches or notes): metal ore is extracted by mining or quarrying [1]. The metal is refined using heat [1], chemical reactions [1] or electrolysis [1]. The metals are then usually melted [1] and either cast into products [1] or mechanically shaped [1].
6. a) Non-ferrous [1]
   b) Any suitable application [1]
   c) Stainless steel [1]
   d) Copper [1]
   e) Any one of: low friction, corrosion resistant. malleable [1]
   f) Any one of: locks, bearings, musical instruments [1]

**Materials: Polymers**

7. a) Any one of: epoxy resin, polyester resin, urea formaldehyde, melamine formaldehyde, phenol formaldehyde [1]
   b) Any typical application [1]
   c, e) Any one of: PET, HDPE, PVC, HIPS, PP, PMMA [1]
   d, f) Any typical application [1]
8. Award up to 4 marks as follows: a thermoforming polymer softens when heated [1] and can be reshaped [1], whereas the form of a thermosetting polymer does not change with temperature [1] and when heated it may start to char. In a thermosetting polymer the polymer chains are permanently interlinked with chemical bonds [1].

**Materials: Textiles**

9. Award up to 4 marks as follows (information can be in either sketches or notes).
   - Knitted fabrics are made from interlocking loops [1] whereas woven fabrics are constructed from interlaced yarns [1].
   - Knitted fabrics have greater elasticity than woven fabrics [1].
   - Woven fabrics have a grain due to the direction of the threads [1] and a selvedge (an edge that will not fray when cut) [1].
   - Any other relevant point.
10. 10.1) Award up to 4 marks as follows: it is made up of carbon atoms [1] arranged hexagonally in a flat 2D layer just one atom thick [1]. It is about 200 times stronger than steel [1], flexible [1], transparent [1] and conducts heat and electricity well [1].
    10.2) Award 1 mark each for up to three suitable applications; for example solar cells [1], touch panels [1] and smart windows for phones [1].

**Materials: New Materials**

11. 11.1) A material made up of particles that are less than 100 nanometres in size [1].
    11.2) 1 mark for stating an application, and 1 mark for a suitable reason or function. For example, as a coating on fabric [1] to repel dirt, keeping it clean [1].
12. 12.1) Award 1 mark each for any two of: nuts and bolts, screws, hinges, fasteners, caps, washers.
    12.2) Award 1 mark each for any two of: resistors, dual in-line integrated circuit packages (DIL), microcontrollers (for example PICs), capacitors, diodes, LEDs, transistors, switches, motors.
    12.3) Award 1 mark each for any two of: gears, cams, pulleys, belts.

**Finishing Materials**

13. For each material type award 1 mark for each correct finishing type. For example:
    - Paper and board: printing [1], embossing [1]
    - Timber-based materials: painting [1], varnishing [1]
    - Metal-based materials: dip-coating [1], galvanising [1].
14. To improve function and aesthetics [1].

**Selection of Materials**

15. Award 1 mark each for stating two relevant properties and a second mark each for explaining why it is required, up to a maximum of 4 marks. Examples of properties which may be considered include the following.

# Answers

| Promotional flyer | Ability to be printed<br>Availability<br>Cost |
|---|---|
| Wooden toy | Aesthetics: colour and texture that appeal to children<br>Absorbency and resistance to corrosion, in case put in child's mouth<br>Toughness, to resist impacts or being dropped<br>Hardness, to resist being scratched or damaged in use |
| Cooking pan | Thermal conductivity, to allow heat through<br>Absorbency and resistance to corrosion, to resist tainting the contents<br>Malleability for ease of manufacture<br>Hardness to avoid being scratched or worn when in use<br>Density, lightweight to lift easily |
| Plastic chair | Compressive strength to support the person sitting on it<br>Absorbency and resistance to corrosion, to resist damage by rain if used outside<br>Density, lightweight so can be lifted easily and put away |
| Football shirt | Aesthetics: colour and texture that appeal to the user<br>Elasticity/stretchiness to provide a good fit/shape<br>Density, lightweight to avoid additional load on wearer |
| Gearbox | Toughness so it does not break on impact in an accident<br>Density, lightweight to reduce fuel requirements<br>Absorbency and resistance to corrosion, so that it doesn't stop working in wet weather<br>Hardness of mechanical parts, so they last a long time before wearing out |

16. Award 1 mark each for stating three methods and a second mark each for describing what it involves or how it provides reinforcement. For example:
    - Bending and folding [1] increase the effective thickness of sheet material [1].
    - Lamination [1] involves adding layers of material [1].
    - Webbing [1] uses ribs of material, normally located on the inside of a product to increase the stiffness.
    - Interfacing [1] involves adding extra layers of material to a textile product [1].

## Pages 92–107 Revise Questions

**Page 93 Quick Test**
1. A group of identical products are made together, before changing to making a group of a different product.
2. For example cars, nuts and bolts
3. The standard shapes and sizes in which a material is available

**Page 95 Quick Test**
1. Scissors, scalpels, craft knives, compass cutters and circle cutters, rotary trimmers and guillotines
2. Adding additional layers to a material
3. Screen printing, offset lithography

**Page 97 Quick Test**
1. Tenon, coping, band saw, circular saw (also powered fretsaw and jigsaw)
2. Polyvinyl adhesive (PVA)
3. Steam bending, laminating using a former

**Page 99 Quick Test**
1. Centre lathe
2. Adhesive/epoxy resin, welding, brazing
3. To allow air to escape when the molten metal is poured in

**Page 101 Quick Test**
1. Coping saw, powered fretsaw, band saw
2. Heat from an electrically heated welding gun or a hot plate is used to melt the faces to be joined, which are pushed together to form the joint as they cool.
3. In injection moulding the formed part is solid; in blow moulding, the output from the injection moulding unit is a pipe, which is expanded within the mould using air to create a hollow product.

**Page 103 Quick Test**
1. A strip of adhesive web is placed between the two fabrics. Heat from an iron then fuses them together.
2. Make a single or double fold and add stiches at the top or side to hold it in place.
3. Manual soldering, reflow (flow) soldering.

**Page 105 Quick Test**
1. A reference point for measurement on a material, product or object
2. To ensure accuracy and precision of manufacture.
3. To ensure that all parts of a product are made the same.
4. A type of template that is used to trace the parts of a garment onto fabric before it is cut. Or, a replica of a product to be cast, used to prepare the cavity into which the molten material will be poured.

**Page 107 Quick Test**
1. Accuracy is the degree of closeness of a measurement to its true value, correct value or standard. Precision is how repeatable or reproducible the measurement is.
2. To ensure that a product is fit for purpose.
3. The permissible limits of variation in the dimensions or physical properties of a manufactured product or part.
4. Quality control is product-oriented whereas quality assurance is process-oriented.

## Pages 108–115 Review Questions

**Properties of Materials**
1. 1.1) Hardness [1]
   1.2) Thermal conductivity [1]

**Materials: Paper and Board**
2. Award marks as indicated, with up to 2 marks for each characteristic and 1 mark for a typical use.

| Type | Characteristics | Typical Use |
|---|---|---|
| Layout and tracing paper | Hard [1] and translucent [1]<br>Typically 50–90 gsm [1] | Working drawings [1], tracing [1] |
| Solid white board | Strong [1], white [1]<br>Made from pure bleached wood pulp [1]<br>200–400 gsm [1] | For example book covers [1], expensive packaging [1] |
| Corrugated cardboard | Contains two or more layers of card with interlacing fluted inner section [1]<br>Often made from recycled material [1], low cost [1]<br>From 250 gsm upwards [1] | For example boxes [1], packaging [1] |
| Foil-lined board | Made by laminating aluminium foil to one side of another board [1]<br>Insulating properties [1], can keep moisture in/out [1] | For example drinks cartons [1], ready meal lids [1] |

# Answers

**Materials: Timber**

3. Award marks as indicated, up to a maximum of 4 marks: hardwoods come from deciduous trees [1] which shed their leaves each autumn [1]. Softwoods come from coniferous trees [1] which keep their leaves all year [1], meaning that they typically grow faster than hardwoods [1]. Softwoods also tend to have a more open grain than hardwoods [1].

4. Award up to 4 marks as follows (information can be in either sketches or notes): trees are cut down [1] and layers of veneer/plies are shaved from them [1]. These are glued together [1] with the grain structure at 90° to each other [1].

**Materials: Metal**

5. 5.1) A mixture of two or more metals [1]
   5.2) i) For example stainless steel [1], high-speed steel [1]
      ii) 1 mark for any of: (for stainless steel) kitchen equipment, medical instruments or any other suitable application; (for HSS) drill bits, saw blades.
      iii) 1 mark each for identifying a requirement of the application and justifying the choice with respect to one of the material properties (for example tough, strong, hard, difficult to machine, corrosion resistant).
   5.3) i) Any suitable non-ferrous alloy, for example brass [1]
      ii) 1 mark for any appropriate application.
      iii) 1 mark each for identifying a requirement of the application and justifying the choice with respect to one of the material properties.

**Materials: Polymers**

6. Award marks as indicated up to a maximum of 10 marks: most polymers are made from carbon-based fossil fuels [1] such as oil, gas and coal [1]. These are a finite resource [1] and non-renewable: once they are used they are gone [1]. The extraction of these resources and their transportation can also cause damage to the environment [1]. Sustainable polymers are being developed from vegetable products [1], such as corn starch [1]. Synthetic polymers are not normally biodegradable [1]. At the end of their usable life, thermosetting polymers typically end up in landfill [1], which uses up valuable land [1] and can be a cause of pollution [1] and damage to local habitats [1]. Thermoforming polymers can be recycled [1]. They are normally marked with a symbol to identify their type [1] and they must be sorted before recycling [1]. Any other appropriate response.

**Materials: Textiles**

7. Natural fibres come from animals or plants [1], whereas synthetic fibres are made by people, usually from oil [1].

8. 8.1) Home use = 12% of £40 million = 0.12 × 40 = £4.8 million [1 mark for method, 1 mark for answer]

   8.2) Clothing = $\frac{15}{100} = \frac{3}{20}$ [1]

**New Materials and Standard Components**

9. A material made by combining two or more different materials [1] where the two materials remain physically distinct within the structure/are not combined chemically/are only joined mechanically [1].

10. 10.1) Award marks as follows:
      Cost of polymer = 0.4 × £3 = £1.20 [1]
      Total cost = £1.20 + (8 × 0.02) + (2 × 0.32) = £2.00 [1 mark for method, 1 mark for answer]
   10.2) Award marks as follows:
      Total cost = £2 + £2.48 + £1.72 = £6.20 / product [1]
      Allowing for 20% profit, selling price = cost × 1.2 = £7.50 per product [1 mark for method, 1 mark for answer]

**Finishing Materials**

11. For each material type award 1 mark for each correct finishing type. For example:
    - polymers: polishing [1], vinyl decals [1]
    - textile-based materials: printing [1], dyeing [1]
    - electronic and mechanical systems: PCB lacquering [1], lubrication [1].

**Selection of Materials**

12. Award 1 mark each for up to six of the following: functionality, aesthetics, environmental considerations, availability of materials, cost, social factors, ethical considerations, cultural factors.

13. Award 1 mark for stating the modification and 1 mark for stating how this will affect the properties of the material. For example:
    - Paper and board: additives [1] can be added to prevent moisture transfer [1].
    - Timber: seasoning [1] can reduce warping [1], increase strength [1] and hardness [1].
    - Metal alloys: annealing [1] can be used to increase the malleability [1]; anodizing [1] can improve the hardness of aluminium [1].
    - Polymers: chemical additives [1] can reduce UV degradation [1].
    - Textiles: flame retardants [1] reduce fire hazards by making the fabric more difficult to set on fire [1].
    - PCB board: photosensitive board [1] can be used to mask areas that have been exposed to light when the board is etched by chemicals [1].

**Working with Materials**

14. Award 1 mark each for any of: using a stronger material, increasing the thickness of a material, bending or folding, laminating, use of webbing, interfacing.

## Pages 116–121 Practice Questions

**Scales of Manufacture, and Manufacturing Processes 1 and 2**

1. Award 1 mark for each suitable example given. For example: one off: tailored suit, satellites; batch: furniture, clothes for high street stores; mass: chocolate bars, bottles, cars; continuous: steel, oil, chemicals.

2. Award marks as follows: metal blades are positioned in the shape to be cut [1]. They are pushed into the card [1]. Foam rubber around the blade compresses during cutting and pushes to release the cut material [1].

3. a) Making straight cuts [1]
   b) Reducing the size of a piece of timber [1]
   c) Creating deep holes for joints [1]
   d) Turning a round section [1]
   e) Planing end grain [1]
   f) Making grooves and edge profiles [1]

4. Laminating [1], steam bending [1].

5. Horizontal paring cleans out unwanted material [1] by cutting across a joint [1], whereas vertical paring shapes the end of a piece of wood [1] by pushing down onto the waste surface [1].

**Manufacturing Processes 3: Metals and Alloys**

6. Metal shears [1], guillotine [1].

7. Award up to 3 marks as follows (information can be in either sketches or notes): the work piece is held in a chuck [1] and rotated [1]. The cutting tool is moved into the workpiece [1]; it can be moved left and right along the length and in or out to achieve different radii [1].

8. Award up to a maximum of 4 marks as follows: a reusable metal mould is made [1]. Molten metal is poured into a cylinder/into the die-casting machine [1]. A ram then forces this metal into the mould [1]. Pressure is held until the metal solidifies and cools [1]. The mould is then opened and the component removed [1].

**Manufacturing Processes 4: Polymers**

9. 9.1) Award marks as follows: the faces to be joined are heated [1] using an electrically heated welding gun or a hot plate [1]. When these melt [1] they pushed together [1], forming the joint as they cool [1].
   9.2) Solvent cement [1].

10. Award marks as follows (information can be in either sketches or notes): a thermoplastic sheet is heated in an oven until it is flexible [1]. It is then pressed between two moulds [1]. The moulds are male mould and female yoke [1]. It is allowed to cool and hardens into the shape of the mould [1].

# Answers

## Manufacturing Processes 5: Textiles and Electronic Systems

11. **11.1)** Award 1 mark each for any two of: rotary cutter, scissors, pinking shears.
   **11.2)** Award marks as follows: it allows a garment to increase fullness or widen out, modifying the shape [1]. It allows a longer piece of fabric to be attached within the length of a shorter piece [1]
   **11.3)** Award up to two marks as follows: quilting creates surface texture [1] by sandwiching wadding or stuffing between layers of fabric [1] and stitching through the layers [1].
12. Award up to 4 marks as follows: the component is placed through the holes in the circuit board, legs to the copper track side [1]. A small amount of solder is applied to the soldering iron, called 'tinning' [1]. The soldering iron is used to heat the point where the component comes through the board for 2–3 seconds [1]. Solder is fed onto the heated area [1] where it melts and forms the joint [1].

## Measurement and Production Aids, and Ensuring Accuracy

13. 9–12 marks: thorough knowledge and understanding of how accuracy can be ensured when manufacturing products. All points fully explained. Several relevant examples presented to support answer. 5–8 marks: good knowledge and understanding of how accuracy can be ensured when manufacturing products. Majority of points explained. Some relevant examples presented to support answer. 1–4 marks: limited knowledge or understanding. Mainly descriptive response. Few or no relevant examples presented to support answer.
   Indicative answer: accurate measuring and marking out results in parts/products that are cut more accurately. Datums should also be worked to. Tools such as jigs, templates and patterns can be used to ensure accuracy. For example, a jig can be set up to hold and guide a drill, thus ensuring holes are drilled in the same place on each piece of material. A template can be drawn round to ensure a part is produced exactly the same each time it is cut. Tolerances are shown on drawings and/or specifications. They should be followed to ensure the product/part is produced within these permissible limits of variation.

## Pages 122–127 Revise Questions

### Page 123 Quick Test
1. A way for people to raise awareness and money for a project or idea, where people donate money in return for rewards
2. A business or organisation that is run jointly by and for the benefit of its members
3. Less employment for people/change in job roles/retraining of staff to fill different roles

### Page 125 Quick Test
1. Computer-aided design, computer-aided manufacture
2. An approach to improve efficiency of manufacture through the elimination of waste
3. Technology push is where products are developed because of new materials or technologies becoming available, whereas market pull is where products are developed due to market forces.

### Page 127 Quick Test
1. Finite resources are resources that will eventually run out. Non-finite resources are resources that are easy to replenish.
2. Through efficient working practices
3. So that products do not cause offence or upset

## Pages 128–133 Review Questions

### Scales of Manufacture, and Manufacturing Processes 1 and 2
1. **1.1)** Award marks as indicated: a group of identical products are made together [1], followed by other groups of similar (but not necessarily identical) products [1].
   **1.2)** Award 1 mark each for three suitable examples. For example chairs, tables, clothes for high street stores, fire extinguishers, etc.
2. Award marks as follows up to a maximum of 5 marks (information can be in either sketches or notes). The image to print is in relief on the printing plate [1]. Ink is applied, which is attracted to the image [1]. The plate is dampened, which repels ink from any non-image areas [1]. The printing plate transfers an inked image onto the rubber blanket cylinder [1]. The rubber blanket cylinder presses the image onto the paper or card as it's fed through [1].
3. Award 1 mark each for stating three safety precautions and 1 mark each for stating three relevant hazards. For example:
   * eye goggles [1] to protect against swarf/flying debris [1]
   * machine guard [1] to protect against entanglement in the rotating chuck [1]
   * spring-loaded chuck key [1] so this is not accidentally left in the machine and ejected in use [1]
   * using a machine vice or clamp to hold the workpiece [1] to stop it spinning and cutting the user [1].
4. Award up to 5 marks as follows: the timber is heated in steam [1] until it becomes pliable [1]. It is then shaped round a former [1]. It must be clamped in place until it is cool [1] when it will retain the shape of the former [1].

### Manufacturing Processes 3: Metals and Alloys
5. Award 1 mark each for two of: manual bending using a former; feeding the sheet between rollers moving at different speeds; using a press.
6.
   a) Hacksaw [1]
   b) Centre lathe [1]
   c) Drill [1]
   d) Milling machine [1]
7. Award marks as indicated up to a maximum of 4 marks: die casting uses a reusable metal mould [1] which is much more expensive than a mould made from sand [1]. Even though in sand casting a new mould has to be made every time [1], for a batch of 10 products the total cost will probably be less than the cost of the metal mould [1]. Further, the equipment cost for sand casting is much less than for die casting [1].

### Manufacturing Processes 4: Polymers
8. Award 1 mark each for two of: coping saw, (powered) fretsaw, jigsaw, band saw.
9. Award up to 4 marks as follows: a CAD model of the product is produced [1]; this is split into multiple layers by a computer [1]; the 3D printer deposits one layer of material [1], then moves up to deposit the next layer, until the product is complete [1].
10. Award up to 4 marks as follows: a split mould is made in the shape of the bottle [1]. Air is blown into an extruded section of plastic tube [1]. The air forces plastic to the sides of the mould [1]. The mould is then cooled and the product is removed [1].

### Manufacturing Processes 5: Textiles and Electronic Systems
11. To provide a professional finish to seams and hems/to provide a decorative finish [1].
12. Award up to 4 marks as follows: it is used to apply patterns or images to long lengths of fabric [1]. Ink is applied to a series of different rollers in contact with the fabric [1]. Each roller has a pattern/image and normally applies a different colour [1]. The fabric moves continuously [1].
13. Award up to 6 marks as follows: in manual soldering, components are pushed through the circuit board [1] and heat is applied by a soldering iron [1] before the solder is added [1]. The soldered joint is formed on the reverse of the circuit board [1]. In flow soldering components are mounted on top of the circuit board [1] after solder paste is applied [1] and the whole assembly is heated [1]. The soldered joint is formed on the same side of the circuit board as the component [1].

**Measurement and Production Aids, and Ensuring Accuracy**

14. **14.1)** Up to 2 marks for each definition.
   - Jig: a custom tool **[1]** for making sure parts of a product are exactly the same **[1]**.
   - Tolerance: the permissible limits of variation **[1]** in the dimensions of a manufactured product **[1]**.
   **14.2)** Up to 3 marks for explanation. For example: failure to use tolerances could result in improper fits **[1]**, which would result in the product being rejected by clients/stakeholders **[1]**. This would add extra cost and time as the product would need to be remade **[1]**.

## Pages 134–135 Practice Questions

**Impact on Industry, and Impact on Society and Environment**

1. **1.1)** 1 mark for correct answer: a.
   **1.2)** Up to 2 marks for explanation and 1 mark for suitable example. For example: so as not to cause offence/confusion **[1]** as some colours/logos/symbols mean different things in different cultures **[1]**. For example, red is considered good luck in China but symbolises danger in western cultures **[1]**.
   **1.3)** Up to 2 marks for explanation of one benefit. For example: reduction in time taken to manufacture products **[1]** due to reducing waiting time/time when no activity is taking place **[1]**.

**Impact on Production**

2. 1 mark for each suitable advantage and disadvantage. For example:
   - Advantages: increased accuracy of design **[1]**, easier to make changes to design **[1]**, complex designs can be created quickly **[1]**.
   - Disadvantages: initial cost of software can be high **[1]**, requires access to suitable ICT hardware **[1]**.

## Pages 136–137 Review Questions

**Impact on Industry, and Impact on Society and Environment**

1. **1.1)** 1 mark for each advantage and 1 mark for any suitable disadvantage. For example:
   - Advantages: increased efficiency **[1]**, better product quality **[1]**.
   - Disadvantage: reduced employment opportunities for people **[1]**.
   **1.2)** Up to 2 marks for description of difference. For example: finite resources are non-renewable/will run out **[1]**. Non-finite resources are renewable/will not run out **[1]**.

**Impact on Production**

2. 1 mark for each suitable advantage and disadvantage. For example:
   - Advantages: consistency of production **[1]**, high levels of manufacturing accuracy **[1]**, high speed of manufacture **[1]**.
   - Disadvantages: initial cost of machinery can be high **[1]**, time/cost of training staff to use machinery **[1]**.

## Pages 138–147 Mix Exam-Style Questions

1. **1.1)** Award marks as follows up to a maximum of 5 marks (information can be in either sketches or notes): plastic powder or granules are fed from a hopper into the machine **[1]**. Heaters melt the plastic **[1]**. A screw moves the plastic along towards the mould **[1]**. The screw provides pressure on the plastic, forcing it into the mould **[1]**. Pressure is maintained on the mould until it has cooled enough to be opened **[1]**.
   **1.2)** Material needed = $20\,000 \times 2.4 \times 10^{-5} = 0.48$ m³ **[1]**; material lost = $0.5 - 0.48 = 0.02$ m³ or $20 \times 10^{-3}$ m³ **[1]**
   **1.3)** Profit = $8.00 - 6.40 = £1.60$ **[1]**; % profit = $1.60 / 8.00 \times 100/1 = 20\%$ **[1]**
2. Award marks as follows up to a maximum of 10 marks (information can be in either sketches or notes). A pattern is made, normally in wood **[1]**. This is sandwiched between two boxes of oiled sand **[1]**. The boxes are called the cope and the drag **[1]**. The sand is compressed around the pattern **[1]**. The cope and drag are carefully separated and the pattern removed, leaving a hollow shape when they are reassembled **[1]**. There will be a hole for a runner, to allow the metal to be poured in **[1]**. There will also be a hole for a riser, to let air escape **[1]**. The metal is melted **[1]**. Metal is poured in through the runner **[1]**. Once the metal has cooled, the sand mould can be broken/shaken off **[1]**. The runner and riser can be cut off **[1]**. Any excess metal/flash will be removed and the casting trimmed or cleaned by fettling **[1]**.
3. **a)** Award 1 mark for tenon saw.
   **b)** Award 1 mark for cutting circles.
   **c)** Award 1 mark for metal.
   **d)** Award 1 mark for paper and card.
   **e)** Award 1 mark for cutting straight lines.
   **f)** Award 1 mark for pinking shears.
   **g)** Award 1 mark for centre lathe.
4. **4.1)** 1 mark for each appropriate input and output, such as LDR (input) and lamp (output).
   **4.2)** Up to 2 marks for each reason explained. For example: a single microcontroller could replace a whole timing circuit **[1]**, leading to a smaller product **[1]**. Microcontrollers can be reprogrammed **[1]**, so the time period of the light could be shortened if the child gets less scared of the dark **[1]**.
5. **a)** Push–pull linkage **[1]**
   **b)** Rotary **[1]**
   **c)** Linear **[1]**
   **d)** Reciprocating **[1]**
6. Award up to 6 marks as follows: spur gears would allow greater torque **[1]**, as with a pulley and belt high torque may cause the belt to slip **[1]**. The pulley and belt may weigh less than the gears **[1]** as the gears would have to be large enough to mesh/touch **[1]** whereas the pulleys could be small and only connected by the belt **[1]**. The belt on the pulley system could stretch to absorb shocks **[1]**, which could otherwise damage the gears **[1]**. The pulley and belt may be easier to manufacture than the gears **[1]**, which could mean that it costs less **[1]**. Any other appropriate response.
7. **7.1)** Up to 4 marks for explanation. For example: make the product easy to disassemble **[1]** so that the materials/components could be reused in a different product **[1]**. Make the product easy to repair **[1]** so it does not have to be thrown away when a component fails **[1]**.
   **7.2)** Up to 2 marks for correct definition. For example: the total distance that a product travels **[1]** from its place of manufacture to where it is used **[1]**.
   **7.3)** Up to 2 marks for explanation. For example: oceanic pollution can cause death to marine life **[1]** as a result of the harmful chemicals/industrial waste being deposited there **[1]**.
8. **a)** Reciprocating **[1]**
   **b)** Oscillating **[1]**
   **c)** Rotary **[1]**
   **d)** Linear **[1]**
9. **9.1)** Second order **[1]**
   **9.2)** Mechanical advantage = $(40 + 80) / 40 = 3$ [1 mark for method, 1 mark for correct answer]
10. **10.1)** Suppliers deliver materials only when they are needed/about to be used **[1]**.
   **10.2)** Reduces the amount of storage space needed **[1]**; less chance of stock being damaged **[1]**; less wasted materials **[1]**.
11. Award marks as follows up to a maximum of 5 marks (information can be in either sketches or notes). Plastic powder or granules are fed from a hopper into the machine **[1]**. Heaters melt the plastic **[1]**. A screw moves the plastic along towards the mould **[1]**. The screw provides pressure on the plastic, turning

# Answers

it into a continuous stream [1]. The pressure forces the plastic through a die in the profile of the tube, creating the pipe [1].

12. 1 mark for each computer-based tool. Up to 2 marks for explanation of use of each. For example: CAD software [1]: used to create 3D models of products [1] which allows them to be simulated before a physical prototype is produced [1]. Presentation software [1]: used to present initial design ideas to the client [1] so they can give feedback [1].

13. 13.1) Up to 2 marks for each advantage and any disadvantage explained. For example:
   - Advantage 1: less storage space is needed [1] as raw materials are only purchased when they are needed [1].
   - Advantage 2: waste is reduced [1] as materials are not damaged while in storage [1].
   - Disadvantage: there is a risk that raw materials will run out [1] as not as much is kept in storage [1].

   13.2) Up to 2 marks for explanation of purpose. For example: to reduce waste [1] by eliminating activities that consume resources without adding value [1].

# Glossary

**Absorbency** the ability of a material to draw in moisture
**Accuracy** the degree of closeness of a measurement to its true value
**Adhesive** a chemical used to stick or glue objects together
**Aesthetics** how a product appeals to the five senses; its sense of beauty
**Alloy** a mixture of two or more metals
**Annotation** adding labels identifying and explaining key features on a drawing
**Anthropometric data** measurements taken from millions of people of different shapes and sizes and placed in charts
**Art Nouveau** a design movement known for its use of long, organic lines and architectural designs
**Arts and Crafts** a design movement that favoured a return to traditional craft methods
**Atmospheric pollution** the release of pollutants into the Earth's atmosphere
**Automation** the use of computer systems and control technology to operate equipment

**Batch production** making a series of groups of identical products
**Battery** converts chemical energy to electrical energy to power products and systems
**Bauhaus** a German design school that existed from 1919 to 1933 and favoured a minimalist approach to design
**Biodegradable** the ability to decompose or rot due to interaction with the environment
**Biomass** fuel that is developed from organic materials, such as crops, scrap wood and animal waste
**Blow moulding** a process used to shape hollow polymer products
**Bonding** a method of joining fabrics without stitching
**Brazing** a joining process for metals where a joint is created by soldering at high temperature
**Breadboarding** a temporary, physical method for prototyping electronic circuits

**Cam** a mechanism that converts rotary motion to reciprocating motion
**Casting** pouring molten metal into a mould to form a product
**CNC** computer numerical control; using a computer to control a machine tool
**Composite** a material made up of two or more other materials that are not chemically combined
**Computer-aided design (CAD)** the use of computer software to produce designs for products
**Computer-aided manufacture (CAM)** the use of computer software to control machine tools to manufacture products
**Continuous improvement** a process where ongoing incremental improvements are made to a product or system
**Continuous production** making a material or chemical continuously using dedicated equipment
**Co-operative** a business or organisation that is run jointly by and for the benefit of its members
**Cracking** a process where complex organic chemicals are broken down into simpler molecules such as the monomers used to make polymers
**Crowd funding** a way for people to raise awareness and money for a project or idea, where people donate money in return for rewards

**Datum surface** a reference point for measurement on a material, product or object
**Deforestation** the removal of forests and conversion of the land to other uses
**Density** mass of material per unit volume
**Design brief** a short description of a design problem and how it is to be solved
**Design fixation** when designers become overly attached to a particular idea, therefore not taking account of other potential solutions

**Design specification** a list of measurable design criteria that a product or system must meet
**De Stijl** a Dutch design movement that simplified designs by using only horizontal and vertical lines, and primary colours
**Die casting** a process where molten metal is shaped using pressure and a reusable mould
**Die cutting** a process that uses metal blades and a press to cut a shape in paper or card
**Ductility** the ability of a material to be stretched without breaking and stay permanently in its new form

**Economies of scale** a saving in cost per product gained by making a higher number of products
**Effort** the force applied to something (for example to a lever)
**Elasticity** the ability of a material to return to its original shape when a force on it is removed
**Electrical conductivity** the ability of electricity to be conducted by a material
**Electronic system** a collection of input, process, driver and output stages that respond to, change and produce different types of signals
**Embossing** a technique that uses steel dies to press a shape onto the material, giving a tactile effect
**End user** the person or people that will use a product when it is completed
**Ergonomics** the study of how people interact with the products and systems around them
**Evaluation** an assessment of how well a product or prototype looks, functions or does its job
**Exploded drawing** a picture that shows how the parts of a product fit together
**Extrusion** making a sectional shape by pushing material through a die

**Fair trade** a movement that works to help people in developing countries get a fair deal for the products that they produce
**'Fast fashion'** a trend where catwalk clothing designs move quickly to the high street so people can capture the current fashions; often clothes will only be worn for a single 'season' before being replaced
**Ferrous metal** a metal that contains iron
**Finite resource** a resource of which there is only a limited quantity
**Former** a profiled shape used to mould material
**Fossil fuel** fuel created from the remains of dead organisms over a long period of time; for example, coal, oil and gas
**Fractional distillation** separation of a liquid mixture into the different chemicals of which it is comprised by a chemical distillation process
**Fulcrum** the pivot point of a lever
**Functionality** how well a product fulfils the purpose it is designed to meet
**Fusibility** the ability of a material to be changed from a solid to a liquid by heat

**Gathering** a sewing technique for shortening the length of a strip of fabric, to allow a longer piece to be attached to a shorter piece
**Gear** a mechanism used to transfer rotary motion, which can also change the direction or magnitude of the force transmitted
**Grain** the growth rings visible on the surface of the wood
**Graphene** a form of carbon consisting of sheets which are one atom thick
**gsm** grams per square metre; the weight of paper or card

**Hardness** the resistance of a material to wear and abrasion
**Hardwood** wood from deciduous trees that shed their leaves each autumn
**Hydro-electrical energy** energy that is taken from flowing water, typically by releasing water from a dam to turn turbines

# Glossary

**Inclusive design**   the design of products and systems that can be used by everyone, without any special adaptations
**Injection moulding**   a process used to shape polymer products
**Input device**   a device that turns a real-world signal, such as light, sound or movement, into an electronic signal
**Interfacing**   adding multiple layers of material to a textile product to increase its strength
**Isometric projection**   a scaled 3D drawing with sides at an angle of 30° to the baseline
**Iterative design**   a cyclic design approach where each iteration is tested, evaluated and refined, resulting in a new iteration

**Jig**   a custom-made tool designed to achieve accuracy, repeatability and interchangeability during product manufacture
**Just-in-time production**   a production technique where suppliers deliver materials only when they are needed

**Knitted**   made from yarn using interlocking loops

**Laminating**   overlaying a flat object or sheet of material with a layer of protective material
**Lean manufacturing**   an approach to improve efficiency of manufacture through the elimination of waste
**Lever**   a simple device that pivots about a fulcrum
**Linear**   moving in a straight line
**Line bending**   a process that involves bending thermoplastic along a heated line
**Linkage**   an assembly of parts used to transfer motion between two mechanisms, which can also change the direction or magnitude of the force transmitted

**Malleability**   the ability of a material for its shape to be permanently changed without the material breaking
**Manufacturing specification**   a set of information that is required to manufacture a product or system
**Market pull**   products developed because of market forces
**Market research**   when information is collected to find out whether there is a place in the market for a proposed product
**Mass production**   making the same product in large quantities
**Mathematical model**   a representation of a product or system using mathematical formulae
**Memphis**   a design movement characterised by the use of asymmetric shapes and colourful decoration
**Metal foam**   a metal containing gas-filled pores, giving it a very low density
**Microcontroller**   a small, programmable computer on a chip that is designed for use in control applications
**Model**   a representation of a product or system that is being developed
**Moisture-wicking fabric**   fabric that removes sweat from the skin and carries it to the outside of the fabric
**Moulding**   using a former to shape a material

**Nanomaterials**   materials made up of particles that are less than 100 nanometres in size
**Natural fibres**   fibres from sources such as animals and plants
**Non-ferrous metal**   a metal that does not contain iron
**Non-renewable energy source**   an energy source that cannot replenish itself quickly and therefore will eventually run out
**Nuclear power**   power that is created by making use of highly controlled nuclear reactions, such as nuclear fission

**Oceanic pollution**   the release of chemicals or industrial waste into the oceans
**Offset lithography**   a transfer printing process used to print products in large quantities

**One-off/bespoke production**   making a single product to a customer specification
**Orthographic projection**   a scale drawing that shows a series of views of a part
**Oscillating**   swinging in alternate directions
**Output device**   a device that turns an electronic signal into a real-world signal, such as light or sound

**Pattern**   a type of template that is used to trace the parts of a garment onto fabric before it is cut; also, a replica of a product to be cast, used to prepare the cavity into which the molten material will be poured
**PCB lacquering**   the application of a waterproof and protective layer for the tracks and pads of a printed circuit board (PCB)
**Perforation**   a hole in a material
**Perspective**   a 3D drawing technique that uses guidelines to show how dimensions change with distance
**Piping**   a strip of folded over fabric inserted in a seam in a textile product
**Pleating**   making a double or multiple fold in a textile product, held by stitching
**Ply**   a layer of paper, wood or fabric in a material
**Polishing**   a finishing technique used to protect and improve the aesthetics of plastics and metals
**Polymer**   a material made from chains of a repeating chemical part called a monomer
**Precision**   how repeatable or reproducible a measurement is
**Presentation software**   software that allows visual aids to be created for face-to-face presentations
**Pressing**   applying pressure to deform a material
**Primary data**   raw data taken first hand or from original research
**Process**   changes an electronic signal to create functions such as timing and counting
**Prototype**   a full-sized, actual version or primary example of an intended product or system
**Pulley**   a mechanism comprising two wheels linked by a belt; this transfers rotary motion and can also change the direction or magnitude of the force transmitted

**Quality assurance**   putting systems in place that ensure the quality of the processes used to manufacture the product
**Quality control**   testing and checking that a product meets the specification or a set of defined quality standards
**Quilting**   sandwiching wadding or stuffing between layers of fabric and stitching through the layers

**Reciprocating**   moving backwards and forwards
**Recycle**   to reprocess or convert waste back into a useful material
**Reinforcement**   adding strength or stiffness to a product
**Renewable energy source**   a source that can replenish itself quickly and therefore will not run out
**Rotating**   turning in a circle

**Scale**   the ratio of the size of a drawn object to the size of the object
**Secondary data**   data that is freely available and taken from other parties or sources
**Selvedge**   an edge of a fabric that will not fray
**Sewing**   a method of joining fabrics by stitching with thread
**Shearing**   a wasting process used to cut material
**Softwood**   wood from trees that maintain their foliage all year round
**Solar energy**   energy that is taken from the sun, typically by using solar panels to harness sunlight and convert it into electricity
**Soldering**   a joining process for metals where a filler metal is melted to join parts together

**Spreadsheet software**   software that presents and allows the analysis of data in tabular form

**Standard component**   a common part that is commercially available in specified sizes

**Stock forms**   the standard shapes and sizes in which a material is available

**Strength**   the ability of a material to withstand a force that is applied to it

**Sustainable**   naturally replenished within a short period of time

**Synthetic**   made by people; not natural

**Synthetic fibres**   fibres made by people, typically from oil or chemicals

**Systems thinking**   a top-down design approach that starts with an overview of the overall system in terms of its input, process and output sub-systems

**Technical textile**   a fabric made for its performance properties rather than aesthetic characteristics

**Technology push**   products developed as a result of developments in materials and/or manufacturing technologies/techniques

**Template**   used to draw a shape onto material which can then be cut around

**Thermal conductivity**   the ability of heat to be conducted through a material

**Thermoforming polymer**   a polymer that can be reshaped when it is heated

**Thermosetting polymer**   a polymer that will not change its shape when reheated

**Toile**   an early version of a piece of clothing, usually made from cheap materials

**Tolerance**   the permissible limits of variation in the dimensions or physical properties of a manufactured product or part

**Toughness**   the ability of a material to absorb an impact without rupturing

**Trend**   a change in direction in the way people are acting or behaving

**Turning**   using a lathe to create a product with a round profile by wasting

**User-centred design**   a design approach where the needs and wants of the end user are considered extensively at each stage of the design process

**Vacuum forming**   a process where heated plastic is formed onto a mould using a vacuum

**Varnishing**   a finishing technique for timber where varnish is applied to protect the wood underneath

**Veneer**   a thin layer of wood

**Virtual meeting software**   software that allows face-to-face meetings to occur between people in different locations over a wired, wireless or mobile network

**Wasting**   removal of material

**Webbing**   ribs of material that provide reinforcement, normally inside a product

**Welding**   a joining process for materials where the parts are melted along the joint line by heat

**Wind energy**   energy that is taken from the wind, typically by using wind turbines to generate electricity

**Working drawing**   a scale drawing that shows the dimensions of a part

**Woven**   made from interlaced yarn

**Yarn**   spun and twisted fibres

# Index

# AQA GCSE Revision

# Design and Technology

## AQA GCSE

### Workbook

## Paul Anderson and David Hills-Taylor

# Contents

## Tools, Equipment and Processes

## New and Emerging Technologies

# Design Strategies

**1** The table shows three design strategies.

Complete the table by giving **one** advantage and **one** disadvantage of using each design strategy.

| Design Approach | Advantage of Strategy | Disadvantage of Strategy |
|---|---|---|
| Iterative design | | |
| User-centred design | | |
| Systems thinking | | |

[6]

**Total Marks** ............... / 6

# Electronic Systems

**1** The table shows different electronic components.

Complete the table by stating whether each component is an input, process or output device and giving an example application of each in a product.

| Component | Input, Process or Output | Application |
|---|---|---|
| Push switch | | |
| Lamp | | |
| Microcontroller | | |
| Thermistor | | |
| Buzzer | | |

[10]

Total Marks _____ / 10

# The Work of Others: Designers

**1** Name a designer that you have studied.

[1]

**2** State a product that the designer given in your answer to question 1 has designed.

[1]

**3** Give **four** features of the design given in your answer to question 2.

1

2

3

4

[4]

Total Marks _____ / 6

# The Work of Others: Companies

**1** Name a design company that you have studied.

........................................................................................................................... [1]

**2** State a product that the company given in your answer to question 1 has designed.

........................................................................................................................... [1]

**3** Give **four** features of the design given in your answer to question 2.

1 ...........................................................................................................................

...........................................................................................................................

2 ...........................................................................................................................

...........................................................................................................................

3 ...........................................................................................................................

...........................................................................................................................

4 ...........................................................................................................................

........................................................................................................................... [4]

**Total Marks** ............... / 6

# Ecological, Environmental and Social Issues

**1** Explain **three** ways that a product can be designed to be more sustainable.

1 ................................................................................................................................................

...................................................................................................................................................

...................................................................................................................................................

...................................................................................................................................................

2 ................................................................................................................................................

...................................................................................................................................................

...................................................................................................................................................

...................................................................................................................................................

3 ................................................................................................................................................

...................................................................................................................................................

...................................................................................................................................................

...................................................................................................................................................

**[6]**

**2** The image shows the Fairtrade Certification mark.

What is meant by the term 'fair trade'?

...................................................................................................................................................

...................................................................................................................................................

...................................................................................................................................................

...................................................................................................................................................

**[2]**

# Research and Investigation

**1** Explain why designers conduct market research.

........................................................................................................................................

........................................................................................................................................

........................................................................................................................................

........................................................................................................................................ [2]

**2** Explain the purpose of a focus group.

........................................................................................................................................

........................................................................................................................................

........................................................................................................................................

........................................................................................................................................ [2]

**3** Give **two** types of data that can be used when investigating a design problem.

1 ....................................................................................................................................

2 .................................................................................................................................... [2]

**4** Which of the following is the correct definition of anthropometric data? Tick one correct box.

**a** Height measurements taken from a small sample of people. ☐

**b** A range of body measurements taken from large numbers of people. ☐

**c** A range of body measurements taken from a small sample of people. ☐

**d** Head measurements taken from millions of people. ☐ [1]

Total Marks ................... / 7

# Briefs and Specifications

**1** A design brief for a new product is shown.

> **Design brief**
>
> Young children learn about the world around them through play.
>
> A local company is designing an educational toy aimed at children aged 4–7.
> The toy must help the children to improve their literacy skills.

Write a **three**-point design specification for a product that would meet the design brief.

Explain why each point is important.

1 ...........................................................................................................................................

...........................................................................................................................................

Explanation ...................................................................................................................

...........................................................................................................................................

...........................................................................................................................................

2 ...........................................................................................................................................

...........................................................................................................................................

Explanation ...................................................................................................................

...........................................................................................................................................

...........................................................................................................................................

3 ...........................................................................................................................................

...........................................................................................................................................

Explanation ...................................................................................................................

...........................................................................................................................................

...........................................................................................................................................

...................................................................................................................... [6]

Total Marks ............ / 6

# Exploring and Developing Ideas

**1** Sketching ideas can be one stage of an iterative design process.

Give **four** other possible stages of an iterative design process.

1 ........................................................................................................................

2 ........................................................................................................................

3 ........................................................................................................................

4 ........................................................................................................ [4]

**2** The image shows a freehand sketch of a product idea.

Explain why designers produce freehand sketches of ideas for products.

........................................................................................................................

........................................................................................................................

........................................................................................................................

........................................................................................................................

........................................................................................................................

........................................................................................................................

........................................................................................................ [4]

# Communication of Ideas 1

**1** A company wants to design a toy car for small children. They have asked you to generate an idea for the design.

**1.1)** On the grid, produce an isometric drawing of your design idea. [4]

**1.2)** Annotate your design to indicate the main features, including:

- sizes

- the materials and finishes to be used

- how it could be made.

[6]

Total Marks _____ / 10

# Communication of Ideas 2

**1** In the space provided, produce a third-angle projection of the following component.

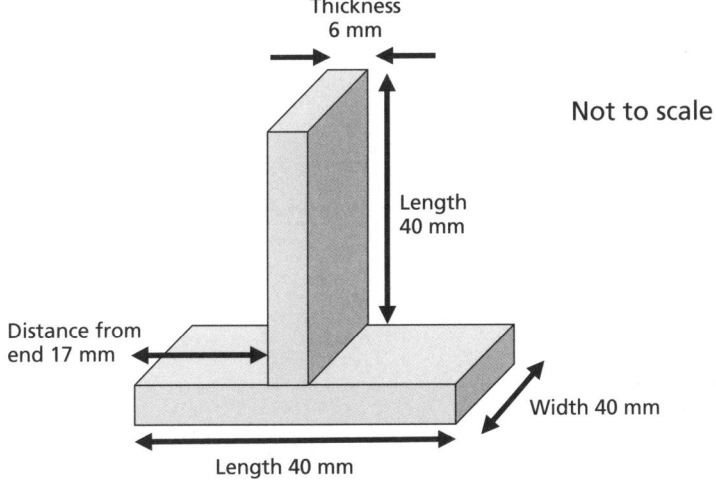

Thickness 6 mm

Not to scale

Length 40 mm

Distance from end 17 mm

Width 40 mm

Length 40 mm

Include all sizes needed to allow manufacture of the component.

[11]

**Total Marks** _____ / 11

# Computer-Based Tools

**1** Complete the table by giving a suitable computer-based tool for completing each task listed.

| Task | Computer-Based Tool |
|---|---|
| Creating a bill of materials for a product that is to be manufactured | |
| Creating a 3D model of a product | |
| Preparing images of a product prototype for inclusion in a face-to-face presentation | |
| Creating visual aids for presentation of a prototype at a focus group meeting | |
| Hosting a virtual meeting | |

[5]

**2** **2.1)** What type of software can be used for creating graphs?

[1]

**2.2)** What type of software can be used for viewing designs from different angles?

[1]

Total Marks ............... / 7

# Prototype Development

**1** Give **two** reasons why designers evaluate prototypes.

1 ................................................................................................................................

................................................................................................................................

2 ................................................................................................................................

................................................................................................................................ [2]

**2** State **six** considerations that designers should take account of when developing prototypes of products or systems.

1 ................................................................................................................................

................................................................................................................................

2 ................................................................................................................................

................................................................................................................................

3 ................................................................................................................................

................................................................................................................................

4 ................................................................................................................................

................................................................................................................................

5 ................................................................................................................................

................................................................................................................................

6 ................................................................................................................................

................................................................................................................................ [6]

Total Marks ................ / 8

# Energy Generation and Storage

**1** The table shows different sources of energy.

Complete the table by stating whether each is renewable or non-renewable and describing how each is used to produce energy.

| Source of Energy | Renewable or Non-Renewable | Description of How Energy is Produced |
|---|---|---|
| Nuclear power | | |
| Solar energy | | |
| Wind energy | | |

[9]

**Total Marks** ............ / 9

# Mechanical Systems 1

**1** State which type of motion is represented by each of the following descriptions.

**1.1)** Swinging backwards and forwards

_____ [1]

**1.2)** Moving straight in one direction

_____ [1]

**1.3)** Moving in a circle

_____ [1]

**1.4)** Moving backwards and forwards

_____ [1]

**2** A first-class lever is being used to raise a load of 60 N. The effort needed to move the load is 24 N.

Calculate how far the load was applied from the fulcrum (length A).

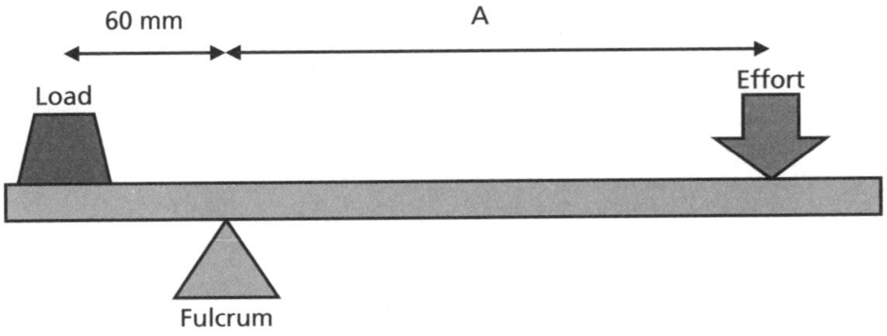

60 mm      A

Load     Effort

Not to scale

Fulcrum

_____

_____

_____

_____

_____

_____ [4]

Total Marks _____ / 8

# Mechanical Systems 2

**1** Describe how the design of a cam can change the motion output from the follower attached to it.

[4]

**2** Two bevel gears similar to those shown are being used in a mechanical device.

Not to scale

The input gear has 48 teeth and rotates at a rate of 60 revolutions per minute (rpm).

If the output gear needs to rotate at a rate of 240 rpm, how may teeth does it need to have?

[4]

Total Marks ........... / 8

# Properties of Materials

**1** State the meaning of the following properties.

**1.1)** Toughness

[1]

**1.2)** Electrical conductivity

[1]

**1.3)** Elasticity

[1]

**2** Name the material property described by each of the following statements.

**2.1)** The ability of a material for its shape to be permanently changed without the material breaking.

[1]

**2.2)** The ability of a material to be changed from a solid to a liquid by heat.

[1]

**2.3)** The ability of a material to draw in moisture, light or heat.

[1]

**3** Explain the difference between a physical property and a working property of a material.

[2]

Total Marks _____ / 8

# Materials: Paper and Board

**1** Explain the differences between duplex board and solid white board.

...................................................................................................................................................................

...................................................................................................................................................................

...................................................................................................................................................................

...................................................................................................................................................................

...................................................................................................................................................................

...................................................................................................................................................................

...................................................................................................................................................................

...................................................................................................................................................................

[4]

**2** A manufacturer has to cut as many copies as possible of the following shape from a piece of foam board.

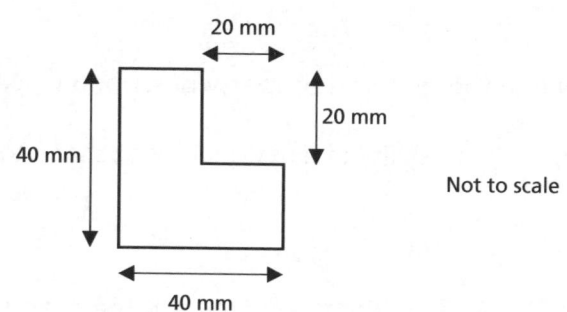

Not to scale

Sketching on the representation of the board shown here, show how you would lay out the shapes to minimise waste.

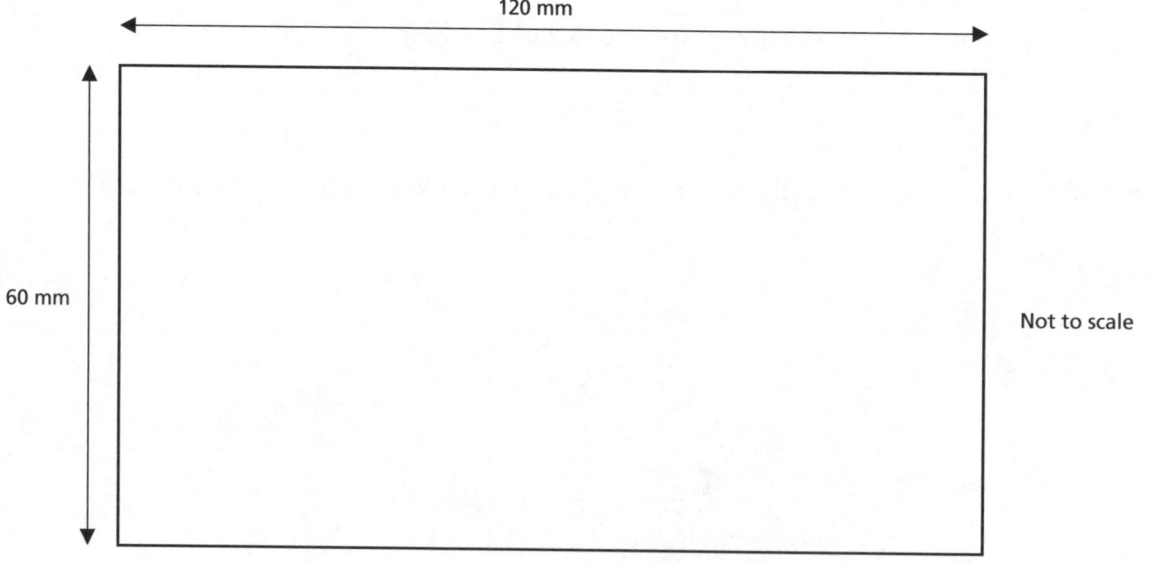

Not to scale

[2]

Total Marks _____ / 6

# Materials: Timber

**1** For each of the timber-based materials listed in the following table, state whether they are a hardwood, a softwood or a manufactured board, and list a typical application.

An example has been completed for you.

| Material | Hardwood, Softwood or Manufactured Board? | Example of Typical Application |
|---|---|---|
| Ash | Hardwood | Tool handles |
| Larch | a) | b) |
| Mahogany | c) | d) |
| Plywood | e) | f) |
| Spruce | g) | h) |
| Balsa | i) | j) |

[10]

**2** Explain what is meant by 'seasoning' wood.

[3]

# Materials: Metals

**1** Name the metallic elements that are the major components of the following metal alloys.

**1.1)** Stainless steel

............................................................................................................................................... [2]

**1.2)** Brass

............................................................................................................................................... [2]

**2** **2.1)** Name **four** stock forms in which metal is commonly available.

1 .........................................................................................................................................

2 .........................................................................................................................................

3 .........................................................................................................................................

4 ......................................................................................................................................... [4]

**2.2)** Explain why a designer may modify a design so that a manufacturer can use metal in stock form.

...............................................................................................................................................

...............................................................................................................................................

...............................................................................................................................................

...............................................................................................................................................

...............................................................................................................................................

............................................................................................................................................... [4]

**3** What is the main difference between ferrous and non-ferrous metals?

...............................................................................................................................................

............................................................................................................................................... [1]

Total Marks ................ / 13

# Materials: Polymers

**1** Using notes and/or sketches, describe how thermoforming polymers are produced from their raw materials.

[4]

**2** A manufacturer is producing solid plastic cubes. Each cube is 30 mm on each side. The manufacturer is using a polymer with a density of 960 kg m$^{-3}$.

Calculate the mass of material needed to make 10 000 cubes. Assume that no material is wasted during the process.

[5]

# Materials: Textiles

**1** **1.1)** Name a natural fibre that is used to make fabric.

........................................................................................................................................................ [1]

**1.2)** Give a typical use for this fabric.

........................................................................................................................................................ [1]

**1.3)** Explain why this fibre is an appropriate choice for this application.

........................................................................................................................................................

........................................................................................................................................................

........................................................................................................................................................

........................................................................................................................................................ [3]

**2** **2.1)** Name a synthetic fibre that is used to make fabric.

........................................................................................................................................................ [1]

**2.2)** Give a typical use for this fabric.

........................................................................................................................................................ [1]

**2.3)** Explain why this fibre is an appropriate choice for this application.

........................................................................................................................................................

........................................................................................................................................................

........................................................................................................................................................

........................................................................................................................................................ [3]

Total Marks .................... / 10

# New Materials

**1** **1.1)** Explain what is meant by a 'smart material'.

........................................................................................................

........................................................................................................

........................................................................................................

[2]

**1.2)** Name a smart material.

........................................................................................................ [1]

**1.3)** Describe the properties of this material that make it 'smart'.

........................................................................................................

........................................................................................................

........................................................................................................

[2]

**1.4)** State an application for which this material is typically used.

........................................................................................................ [1]

**2** **2.1)** Explain what is meant by a 'technical textile'.

........................................................................................................

........................................................................................................ [1]

**2.2)** Name a technical textile and give an application for which it is typically used.

........................................................................................................

........................................................................................................

........................................................................................................

[2]

Total Marks ............ / 9

# Standard Components

**1** Name **two** standard components that are used with each of the following materials.

**1.1)** Paper

1 ................................................................................................................

2 ................................................................................................................ [2]

**1.2)** Fabric

1 ................................................................................................................

2 ................................................................................................................ [2]

**1.3)** Metal

1 ................................................................................................................

2 ................................................................................................................ [2]

**1.4)** Timber

1 ................................................................................................................

2 ................................................................................................................ [2]

**2** Explain why a company may decide to use standard components in a product.

........................................................................................................................

........................................................................................................................

........................................................................................................................

........................................................................................................................

........................................................................................................................

........................................................................................................................

........................................................................................................................

........................................................................................................................ [5]

**Total Marks** ................ / 13

# Finishing Materials

1 The table shows different types of material.

Complete the table by giving **two** finishing techniques that are suitable for use with each type of material.

| Type of Material | Finishing Technique 1 | Finishing Technique 2 |
|---|---|---|
| Papers and boards | | |
| Timber-based materials | | |
| Metal-based materials | | |
| Polymers | | |
| Textile-based materials | | |

[10]

2 Which of the following describes the finishing process of galvanising? Tick the correct box.

a A powder is sprayed onto the metal and then it is heated. ☐

b Air is blown through a powder and then the metal is dipped and heated. ☐

c The metal is dipped into a bath of molten zinc. ☐

d An abrasive liquid is applied to the metal. ☐ [1]

3 What is the purpose of lubricating gears and mechanical parts?

_____

_____ [1]

Total Marks _____ / 12

# Selection of Materials

**1** Choose **one** of the following products by circling your selection:

Food packaging          Flat-pack furniture          Electrical system in a fridge

Plastic socket for an electric plug     Fabric covering for a sofa     Metal hammer

Discuss in detail the properties required by the product you have selected.

[9]

**Total Marks** ......... / 9

# Working with Materials

**1** Explain why a designer may design a product that includes features to provide reinforcement.

[4]

**2** Give **three** examples of different products that include reinforcement to add stiffness.
For each, identify the method of reinforcement used.

Product 1

Product 2

Product 1

[6]

# Scales of Manufacture

**1** Explain how the scale of production affects the cost of a manufactured product.

[10]

# Manufacturing Processes 1: Process Types and Processes used with Paper and Board

**1** The product shown is A6 in size (folded from A5) and includes tear-off tags indicated by the dotted lines. The material available to make it is A1 sheets of duplex board.

**1.1)** Describe the processes that would be used to make a prototype batch of five of the products.

[6]

**1.2)** The final product will be made in batches of 10 000.

Identify a process that could be used to produce the net for the product in a single operation, so it only needs to be folded.

[1]

Total Marks ........... / 7

# Manufacturing Processes 2: Timber-Based Materials

**1** Complete the table, identifying the tools that are typically used to carry out the tasks listed with timber-based materials.

| Task | Tool that is Typically used to Carry Out this Task |
|---|---|
| Making a curved cut in a thin sheet of wood | **a)** |
| Hand smoothing the surface of a flat piece of timber before using abrasives | **b)** |
| Digging out waste material from a groove with sides at an angle of 60° | **c)** |
| Smoothing the surface of an irregularly shaped wooden part | **d)** |
| Turning a circular profile on a block of wood | **e)** |
| Removing large amounts of wood by hand when carving a shape | **f)** |

[6]

**2** Using notes and/or sketches, describe how laminating can be used to make a curved product from natural timber.

[4]

**Total Marks** ............... / 10

# Manufacturing Processes 3: Metals and Alloys

**1** Describe the process of joining two metal parts using welding.

[6]

**2** Explain how brazing is different to welding.

[4]

**3** Name a metal joining technique that does not use heat.

[1]

Total Marks _____ / 11

# Manufacturing Processes 4: Polymers

**1** Using notes and/or sketches, describe how a product is made using vacuum forming.

[10]

**Total Marks** _____ / 10

# Manufacturing Processes 5: Textiles and Electronic Systems

**1** **1.1)** Explain the difference between gathering and pleating.

[2]

**1.2)** Using notes and/or sketches, describe the process of batik.

[5]

**2** Describe the process of reflow (flow) soldering.

[3]

Total Marks _____ / 10

# Measurement and Production Aids

**1** State what is meant by a 'datum surface' when measuring.

[2]

**2** Explain **one** example of how each of the following tools can be used to ensure accuracy of manufacture of a product or part.

Jig

Pattern

[4]

# Ensuring Accuracy

**1** Define the term 'accuracy'.

[2]

**2** Explain what is meant by each of the following.

Quality control

Quality assurance

[4]

Total Marks _____ / 6

# Impact on Industry

1 Explain **one** advantage and **one** disadvantage of increased automation in product manufacture.

Advantage

[4]

2 State what is meant by 'crowd funding'.

[2]

3 Give an example of the use of virtual marketing.

[1]

# Impact on Production

**1** Describe what is meant by 'lean manufacturing'.

[2]

**2** Explain **one** advantage and **one** disadvantage of just-in-time production.

Advantage

Disadvantage

[4]

**3** Describe the difference between market pull and technology push.

[2]

**4** Give **two** examples of CAM equipment.

1

2

[2]

Total Marks / 10

# Impact on Society and the Environment

**1** This question is about the impact of new technologies on society and the environment.

Some elderly people have poor eyesight and therefore can have difficulty using telephones.

Give **two** ways that a telephone could be modified to help elderly people with poor eyesight.

1 ................................................................................................................................

................................................................................................................................

2 ................................................................................................................................

................................................................................................................................ **[2]**

**2** Give **one** positive and **one** potentially negative impact of the increased use of smartphones on society.

Positive impact ...........................................................................................................

................................................................................................................................

Negative impact ..........................................................................................................

................................................................................................................................ **[2]**

**3** Give **one** positive and **one** potentially negative impact of the increased use of smartphones on the environment.

Positive impact ...........................................................................................................

................................................................................................................................

Negative impact ..........................................................................................................

................................................................................................................................ **[2]**

Total Marks ............ / 6

# Collins

## GCSE
# Design and Technology

Time allowed: 2 hours

**Materials**

**For this paper you must have:**

- writing and drawing instruments
- a calculator
- a protractor.

**Instructions**

- Use black ink or ballpoint pen. Only use pencil for drawing.
- Answer all questions.
- Answer the questions in the spaces provided. Do not write on blank pages.
- Do all your rough work in this book and cross through any work that you do not want to be marked.

**Information**

- The marks for questions are shown in brackets.
- The maximum mark for this paper is 100.
- There are 20 marks for Section A, 30 marks for Section B and 50 marks for Section C.

**Name:** ................................................................................................................

# Practice Exam Paper

## Section A

Questions **1–10** are multiple choice questions. You must shade in one lozenge.

**1** You have cut a piece of material to a measurement of 50 × 200 mm. The tolerance allowed is ±1 mm. Which of the following measurements is in tolerance?

**A** 48.9 × 200.6 mm ○

**B** 51.1 × 199.5 mm ○

**C** 49.5 × 199.1 mm ○

**D** 50.3 × 201.5 mm ○ [1 mark]

**2** Which one of the following is a thermosetting polymer?

**A** melamine formaldehyde ○

**B** polypropylene ○

**C** polyvinyl chloride ○

**D** acrylic ○ [1 mark]

**3** Which of the following properties means a material's resistance to abrasion, wear and scratches?

**A** absorbency ⬜

**B** toughness ⬜

**C** hardness ⬜

**D** malleability ⬜ **[1 mark]**

**4** In a gear train similar to the one shown, the large gear has 36 teeth and the small gear has 12 teeth.

If the large gear turns at a rate of 30 revolutions per minute (rpm), what will be the rate of rotation of the small gear?

**A** 10 rpm ⬜

**B** 30 rpm ⬜

**C** 48 rpm ⬜

**D** 90 rpm ⬜ **[1 mark]**

# Practice Exam Paper

**5** An orthographic projection of a part has been drawn to a scale of 1:2. If the length of the part on the drawing is 20 mm, what is the length of the actual part?

**A** 10 mm ◯

**B** 20 mm ◯

**C** 30 mm ◯

**D** 40 mm ◯ **[1 mark]**

**6** Which one of the following is a renewable energy source?

**A** wind ◯

**B** coal ◯

**C** gas ◯

**D** nuclear ◯ **[1 mark]**

**7** Products are sometimes designed as a result of market forces. What is this known as?

**A** Efficient working ◯

**B** Market pull ◯

**C** Quality control ◯

**D** Technology push ◯ **[1 mark]**

**8** Which of the following statements best describes the term 'fair trade'?

   **A**  A business jointly owned and run by its members  ◯

   **B**  A method of marketing and selling a product  ◯

   **C**  A method of raising funding and awareness for a project  ◯

   **D**  A way of ensuring producers of products get a fair deal  ◯  **[1 mark]**

**9** A company has designed a product to fail within 5 years. What is this called?

   **A**  Crowd funding  ◯

   **B**  Planned obsolescence  ◯

   **C**  Quality assurance  ◯

   **D**  Virtual marketing  ◯  **[1 mark]**

**1 0** Which of the following is the use of computers to support designing?

   **A**  CAD  ◯

   **B**  CAM  ◯

   **C**  FMS  ◯

   **D**  JIT  ◯  **[1 mark]**

# Practice Exam Paper

**1 1 · 1** Name a smart material.

_____

**[1 mark]**

**1 1 · 2** Describe the smart property of this material.

_____

_____

_____

_____

**[2 marks]**

**1 1 · 3** Give a typical application for this material.

_____

_____

**[1 mark]**

**1 2** State the stage in an electronic system where each of the following would usually be found.

**1 2 · 1** A buzzer making a sound

_____

**[1 mark]**

**1 2 · 2** A sensor detecting a change in light level

_____

**[1 mark]**

**1 3** Give **two** disadvantages of using non-renewable energy sources.

.......................................................................................................................................

.......................................................................................................................................

.......................................................................................................................................

**[2 marks]**

**1 4** Give **two** advantages of selecting rechargeable batteries instead of non-rechargeable batteries to power products.

.......................................................................................................................................

.......................................................................................................................................

.......................................................................................................................................

**[2 marks]**

# Practice Exam Paper

## Section B

**1 5** The following shape needs to be marked out on a piece of material for cutting.

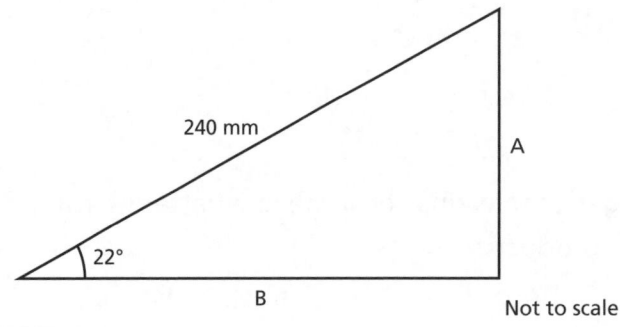

Figure 1

Calculate the length of side A.

_____

_____

_____

_____

**[2 marks]**

**1 6** Choose **one** of the following products. Circle your choice.

Food packaging        Flat-pack furniture        Dessert spoon

Outdoor seat        Wedding dress

**1 6 · 1** Identify **one** specific material that would be suitable for making the product that you have selected.

_____

**[1 mark]**

`1 6` · `2` Explain why this material would be suitable.

[4 marks]

`1 6` · `3` Identify a process that would be suitable for manufacturing your chosen product.

[1 mark]

`1 6` · `4` Describe how this process would be used to manufacture the product.

[5 marks]

# Practice Exam Paper

**1 7** The shape shown needs to be cut out of a sheet of material using nesting to ensure that minimal material is wasted. The measurements are in millimetres. The sheet is 900 mm long by 900 mm wide.

Note: two of these shapes can be nested together to make a simple geometric shape.

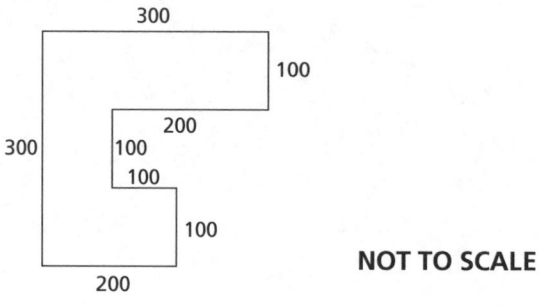

**NOT TO SCALE**

Figure 2

**1 7 · 1** Repeat the shape on the grid to ensure that as many fit on the sheet as possible.

Each box on the grid represents a 100 × 100 mm size.

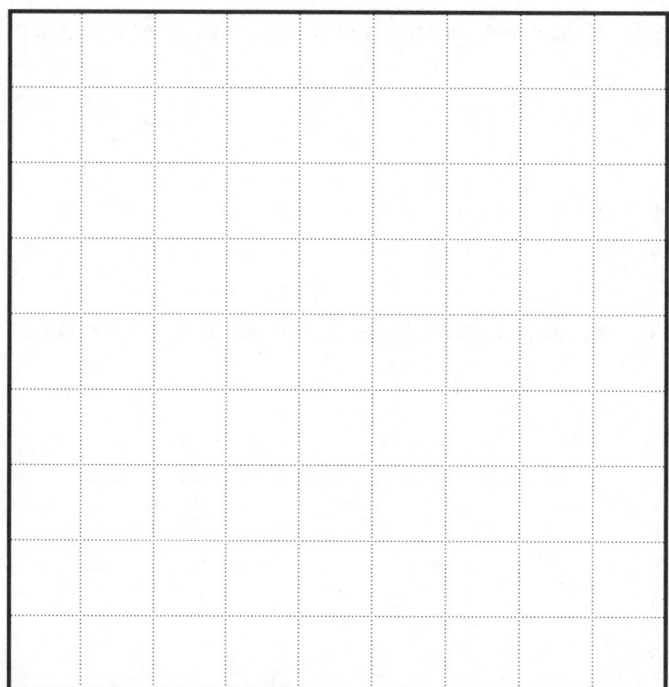

[2 marks]

1 7 · 2 Calculate the surface area of one shape.

**[1 mark]**

1 7 · 3 Calculate the percentage of material wasted when producing the shapes you have drawn above.

**[4 marks]**

# Practice Exam Paper

| 1 | 8 | There are several factors that must be considered when designing and manufacturing products and systems.

Discuss the importance of taking ecological issues into account when designing and manufacturing products and systems.

[10 marks]

# Section C

The product shown is a pair of headphones for listening to music. They are to be worn while exercising. The target market is middle-aged adults.

1 9 · 1 State **four** factors that should be considered when evaluating the headphones.

........................................................................................................................................................

........................................................................................................................................................

........................................................................................................................................................

........................................................................................................................................................

........................................................................................................................................................

**[4 marks]**

1 9 · 2  Evaluate the headphones against **three** of these factors.

1

[4 marks]

2

[4 marks]

3

[4 marks]

**2 0** The headphones shown on page 213 are to be redesigned for use by children aged 6–8 years. They should be suitable for use during a range of different play and learning activities.

**2 0** · **1** Write a **four**-point design specification for the new product. For each point, explain its importance.

1 ............................................................................................................................................................

............................................................................................................................................................

............................................................................................................................................................

**[2 marks]**

2 ............................................................................................................................................................

............................................................................................................................................................

............................................................................................................................................................

**[2 marks]**

3 ............................................................................................................................................................

............................................................................................................................................................

............................................................................................................................................................

**[2 marks]**

4 ............................................................................................................................................................

............................................................................................................................................................

............................................................................................................................................................

**[2 marks]**

# Practice Exam Paper

**2 0 · 2** The designer of the new headphones has decided to look at the work of other designers before sketching a design idea.

Give the name of **two** different designers. For each, explain how their work could influence the design.

1 ................................................................................................................................

................................................................................................................................

................................................................................................................................

**[2 marks]**

2 ................................................................................................................................

................................................................................................................................

................................................................................................................................

**[2 marks]**

2 1 An iterative process was used to design the headphones shown on page 213.

2 1 · 1 Describe the iterative design process.

1 .............................................................................................................................

.............................................................................................................................

.............................................................................................................................

.............................................................................................................................

.............................................................................................................................

.............................................................................................................................

**[4 marks]**

2 1 · 2 Discuss the advantages and disadvantages of using an iterative process to design products.

.............................................................................................................................

.............................................................................................................................

.............................................................................................................................

.............................................................................................................................

.............................................................................................................................

.............................................................................................................................

.............................................................................................................................

.............................................................................................................................

.............................................................................................................................

.............................................................................................................................

**[6 marks]**

# Practice Exam Paper

2 2 Tolerances were considered when manufacturing the headphones.

2 2 · 1 What are tolerances?

_____

_____

_____

**[2 marks]**

2 2 · 2 Explain why tolerances are used in product manufacture.

_____

_____

_____

_____

_____

_____

_____

**[4 marks]**

**2 3** A group of 80 customers was asked to identify the most important characteristic in a new product. Their responses are given in the table.

| Response | Number of Customers | Percentage of Total |
|---|---|---|
| Cost | 36 | 45 |
| Colour | | 25 |
| Surface texture | 8 | |
| Weight | 4 | 5 |
| Undecided/no preference | 12 | 15 |
| **Total** | **80** | **100** |

**2 3 · 1** Insert the missing values in the table.  **[2 marks]**

**2 3 · 2** Use the information in the table to create a bar chart showing the number of customers who like different features. Label your axis with the scale of your graph.

**[2 marks]**

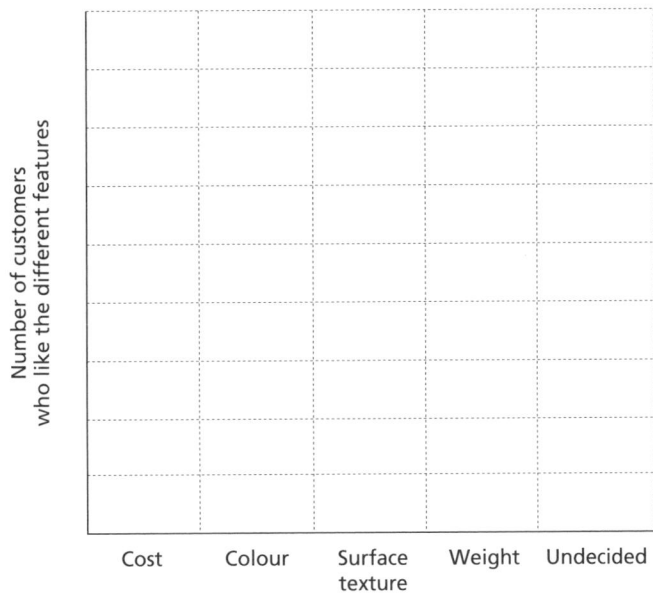

# Practice Exam Paper

**2 3 · 3** Give **two** types of data that can be used when investigating user needs for products.

........................................................................................................................................

........................................................................................................................................

[2 marks]

**END OF QUESTIONS**

# Answers

## Page 164 Design Strategies

1. 1 mark for each suitable response. For example:

| Design Approach | Advantage of Strategy | Disadvantage of Strategy |
|---|---|---|
| Iterative design | Problems with the design can be discovered and dealt with earlier [1]. | It can be time consuming if a lot of prototypes or iterations need to be produced [1]. |
| User-centred design | The end user has a greater ownership of the final product [1]. | The design could become too focused on one particular end user's requirements [1]. |
| Systems thinking | It is easier to find errors or faults in the design [1]. | It can lead to the use of components that are not necessary [1]. |

## Page 165 Electronic Systems

1. 1 mark for stating whether each component is an input, process or output and 1 mark for suitable application of each. For example:

| Component | Input or Output | Application |
|---|---|---|
| Push switch | Input [1] | Starting the timing sequence on a kitchen timer [1] |
| Lamp | Output [1] | Providing light for a bicycle safety light [1]. |
| Microcontroller | Process [1] | Controlling the counting sequence for the score counter on a board game [1] |
| Thermistor | Input [1] | Temperature sensor for an automatic heating system [1] |
| Buzzer | Output [1] | Making a buzzing sound for a doorbell [1] |

## Page 166 The Work of Others: Designers

1. 1 mark for any suitable named designer from the specification. For example: Coco Chanel [1].
2. 1 mark for product designed by designer given in answer to question 1. For example: Chanel Suit [1].
3. 1 mark for each suitable feature of design given in answer to question 2. For example: Chanel suit: masculine/bold look [1], three-piece sleeve [1], machine-quilted lining on jacket [1], made with soft/flexible materials [1].

## Page 167 The Work of Others: Companies

1. 1 mark for any suitable named design company from the specification. For example: Under Armour [1].
2. 1 mark for product designed by company given in answer to question 1. For example: moisture-wicking t-shirt [1].
3. 1 mark for each suitable feature of design given in answer to question 2. For example: moisture-wicking t-shirt: keeps athlete cool [1], removes sweat from body [1], lightweight [1], made using microfibres [1].

## Page 168 Ecological, Environmental and Social Issues

1. Up to 2 marks for explanation of each way. For example: choose recyclable materials [1] so that less new material needs to be sourced [1]. Design for disassembly [1] so that materials/components can be reused [1]. Select a sustainable power supply [1] to reduce reliance on non-renewable energy [1].
2. Up to 2 marks for definition. For example: fair trade is a movement that works to help people in developing countries [1] to get a fair deal for the products that they produce [1].

## Page 169 Research and Investigation

1. Up to 2 marks for explanation. For example: to find out if there is a gap in the market [1] so that a product will be commercially successful [1].
2. Up to 2 marks for explanation. For example: to gain feedback from potential customers [1] to ensure that the product will meet their needs [1].
3. 1 mark for each correct type of data. For example: primary data [1]; secondary data [1].
4. 1 mark for correct answer: b

## Page 170 Briefs and Specifications

1. 1 mark for each specification point and 1 mark for explanation for each. Specification may relate to any suitable product that matches the brief. For example:
   • The product must use bright and attractive colours [1] so it would appeal aesthetically to the child [1].
   • The product must have no sharp edges [1] so as not to cause injury to the child [1].
   • The product must have a set of lettered blocks [1] so that the child can practise making different words [1].

## Page 171 Exploring and Developing Ideas

1. 1 mark for each suitable stage given. For example: modelling [1], testing [1], evaluating [1], improving/refining outcome [1].
2. 1 mark for each reason or 2 marks for each reason explained further, up to a maximum of 4 marks. For example: to get ideas onto paper very quickly [1] as freehand sketches do not have to follow drawing conventions [1]. To share early ideas with potential clients [1] so that they can provide feedback [1].

## Page 172 Communication of Ideas 1

1. 1.1)  Award 1 mark or each of the following:
   • Design appears to be in correct proportion/to scale.
   • Vertical lines/leading edges go straight up.
   • Correct use of guidelines for the horizontal lines.
   • Design is clearly visible as some form of toy car.
   1.2)  Award marks up to a maximum of 6 marks as follows:
   • 1 mark each for two sizes
   • 1 mark each for two materials or one material and one finish; or 2 marks for a material with an explanation of why it is suggested
   • 1 mark each for two identified manufacturing processes; or 2 marks for a manufacturing process with an explanation of why it is suggested.

## Page 173 Communication of Ideas 2

1. Award 1 mark for each of the following, up to a maximum of 11 marks:
   • layout includes three views (top, front, side)
   • top view is accurate representation
   • front view is accurate representation
   • side view is accurate representation
   • views are laid out in correct orientation (top above; front below; side to the right of the front)

- views are aligned with each other
- one to four dimensions listed **[1]**; all five dimensions listed **[2]**
- leader lines are shown to dimensions
- dimension lines are finished with solid arrowheads
- dimensions are located above the line in the centre (or horizontal measurements) or to the left of the line and in the centre (for vertical measurements).

Not to scale

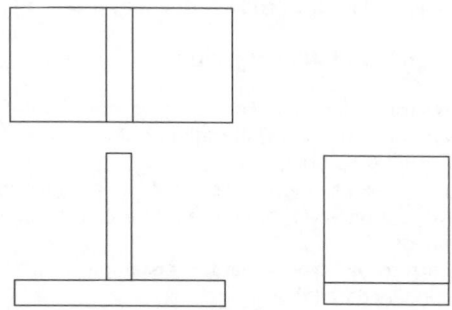

## Page 174 Computer-Based Tools

1. 1 mark for each correct answer – also accept specific items of software if given.

| Task | Computer-Based Tool |
|---|---|
| Creating a bill of materials for a product that is to be manufactured | Spreadsheet software |
| Creating a 3D model of a product | CAD software |
| Preparing images of a product prototype for inclusion in a face-to-face presentation | Image-manipulation software |
| Creating visual aids for presentation of a prototype at a focus group meeting | Presentation software |
| Hosting a virtual meeting | Video conferencing software |

2. **2.1)** Spreadsheet software **[1]**
   **2.2)** CAD **[1]**

## Page 175 Prototype Development

1. 1 mark for each reason. For example: to assess if it is fit for purpose **[1]**. To identify modifications needed **[1]**.
2. 1 mark for each consideration. For example: whether the product is marketable **[1]**; whether it functions correctly **[1]**; whether it is aesthetically pleasing **[1]**; whether it meets the needs of the brief/specification **[1]**; whether it meets the needs of the client **[1]**; whether it is innovative/creative **[1]**.

## Page 176 Energy Generation and Storage

1. 1 mark for stating whether each source of energy is renewable or non-renewable and up to 2 marks for suitable description of how each is used to produce energy. For example:

| Source of Energy | Renewable of Non-Renewable | Description of How Energy is Produced |
|---|---|---|
| Nuclear power | Non-renewable **[1]** | A nuclear reactor creates steam **[1]** which is used to turn turbines **[1]**. *Note: reference must be made to nuclear reactor or nuclear reaction producing steam to gain 1 mark.* |
| Solar energy | Renewable **[1]** | Solar panels collect light from the sun **[1]** and convert it into an electric current **[1]**. |
| Wind energy | Renewable **[1]** | The wind turns turbines **[1]** which then drive generators to produce electricity **[1]**. |

## Page 177 Mechanical Systems 1

1. **1.1)** Oscillating **[1]**
   **1.2)** Linear **[1]**
   **1.3)** Rotating **[1]**
   **1.4)** Reciprocating **[1]**
2. Mechanical advantage = load / effort **[1]** = 60 / 24 = 2.5 **[1]**
   For a first-class lever, mechanical advantage = A / 60
   Rearranging A = mechanical advantage × 60 **[1]** = 2.5 × 60 = 150 mm **[1]**

## Page 178 Mechanical Systems 2

1. Award marks, up to a maximum of 4 marks, as follows: a follower can only rise (go up), dwell (be held at the same height) or fall (go down) **[1]**. How long the follower spends doing each of these depends on the shape of the cam **[1]**. A round section on the cam will provide a dwell **[1]**. The longer the round section, the longer the dwell **[1]**. A snail cam (or similar) will provide a sudden drop **[1]**. Any other relevant point.
2. Gear ratio needed = speed of output gear / speed of input gear **[1]** = 240 / 60 = 4:1 **[1]**
   Number of teeth needed = number of teeth on input gear / gear ratio **[1]** = 48 / 4 = 12 **[1]**

## Page 179 Properties of Materials

1. **1.1)** The ability of a material not to break when a force is applied to it suddenly **[1]**
   **1.2)** The ability of electricity to pass through a material **[1]**
   **1.3)** The ability of a material to return to its original shape when a force is removed **[1]**
2. **2.1)** Malleability **[1]**
   **2.2)** Fusibility **[1]**
   **2.3)** Absorbency **[1]**
3. A physical property is a measurable characteristic of the material itself **[1]** whereas a working property is a reaction to some form of applied force **[1]**.

## Page 180 Materials: Paper and Board

1. Award up to 4 marks as follows. For example: solid white board is made from pure bleached wood pulp **[1]** and is white all the way through **[1]**. Duplex board has white surfaces with grey fibres in between **[1]** and costs less than solid white board **[1]**. It also has slightly less strength **[1]**. The available sizes of duplex board are typically slightly thicker than solid white board **[1]**.
2. Award 1 mark for an attempt to tessellate that is inefficient. Award 2 marks for effective tessellation, for example:

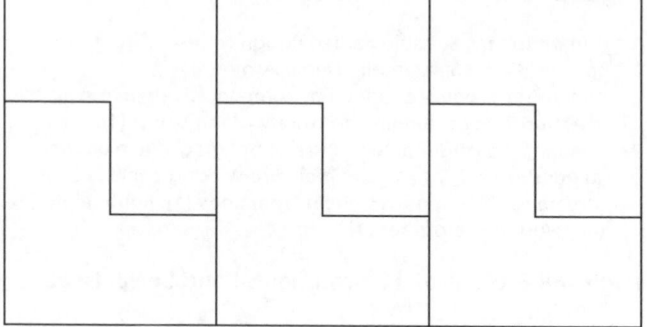

## Page 181 Materials: Timber

1. a) Softwood [1]
   b) Any suitable application. For example: boats and yachts, exterior cladding of buildings, interior panelling [1].
   c) Hardwood [1]
   d) Any suitable application. For example: high-quality furniture [1].
   e) Manufactured board [1]
   f) Any suitable application. For example: furniture, boat building [1].
   g) Softwood [1]
   h) Any suitable application. For example: general construction, wooden aircraft frames [1].
   i) Hardwood [1]
   j) Any suitable application. For example: modelling [1].
2. Seasoning means that the wood is dried before use to remove moisture [1], either in air or by gentle heating in a large kiln [1]. This makes the wood less likely to distort or warp [1].

## Page 182 Materials: Metals

1. 1.1) Award 1 mark each for iron and chromium.
   1.2) Award 1 mark each for copper and zinc.
2. 2.1) Award 1 mark each for up to four of the following: sheet, plate, round bar, square bar, square tube and round tube.
   2.2) Award marks as indicated, up to a maximum of 4 marks. For example: to reform metal it requires much energy [1] and effort [1], and therefore cost [1]. By using a stock form, this cost can be avoided [1].
3. Ferrous metals contain iron; non-ferrous ones do not [1].

## Page 183 Materials: Polymers

1. Award marks as indicated, up to a maximum of 4 marks, for notes or sketches communicating the following content: oil is extracted [1]; this is sent to an industrial refinery [1]; small chemical units called monomers are extracted from the oil [1], which are linked together to form the polymer chains in the polymerisation process [1]. This material can then be extruded/rolled/granulated into the required form [1].
2. Volume of 1 cube = $0.03^3$ [1] = $2.7 \times 10^{-5}$ $m^3$ [1]
   Volume of 10 000 cubes = $2.7 \times 10^{-5} \times 10000 = 0.27$ $m^3$ [1]
   Mass of 10 000 cubes = $0.27 \times 960$ [1] = 259.2 kg [1]

## Page 184 Materials: Textiles

1. 1.1) Award 1 mark for cotton, wool or silk.
   1.2) Award 1 mark for a suitable application. For example: underwear, shirts and blouses, t-shirts or jeans for cotton; jumpers, suits, dresses or carpets for wool; dresses, shirts or ties for silk.
   1.3) Award 1 mark each for up to three properties that make it suitable for the stated application. For example: strong, durable, absorbent for cotton; warm, soft, absorbent, crease resistant for wool; smooth, lustrous and strong for silk.
2. 2.1) Award 1 mark for polyamide/nylon, polyester or elastane/lycra.
   2.2) Award 1 mark for a suitable application. For example: tights and stockings, sportswear, upholstery, carpets for nylon; sportswear for polyester; sportswear, underwear, socks, suits for elastane.
   2.3) Award 1 mark each for up to three properties that make it suitable for the stated application. For example: strong, durable, warm or crease resistant for nylon; strong, durable, elastic, or crease resistant for polyester; high extension and elasticity/stretch for elastane.

## Page 185 New Materials

1. 1.1) A material that has a property that changes in response to its environment [1]. This change is reversible [1].

1.2) Award 1 mark for naming a suitable material, such as: shape memory alloy, thermochromic pigment, photochromic pigment.
1.3) Award 1 mark for stating the property of the material and a second mark for stating the environmental stimulus to which it responds. For example: shape memory alloy reverts to its original shape [1] when heat is applied [1]; thermochromic pigment changes colour [1] in response to temperature [1]; photochromic pigment becomes darker/changes colour [1] in response to increased brightness [1].
1.4) Award 1 mark for naming a suitable application. For example: shape memory alloy: spectacle frames, fire detectors; thermochromic pigment: flexible thermometers, food packaging; photochromic pigment: sunglasses.
2. 2.1) A textile manufactured for performance properties rather than visual appearance [1]
   2.2) Award 1 mark for identifying the technical textile and 1 mark for the application. For example: Kevlar [1] for body armour [1]; fire-resistant fibre [1] used in clothing worn by firefighters [1]; microfibres incorporating micro-encapsulation [1] used for socks and underwear that reduce body odour, or anti-bacterial medical textiles [1]; conductive fibres [1] used to integrate temperature controlled clothing or to integrate lights into emergency clothing [1].

## Page 186 Standard Components

1. 1.1) Award 1 mark each for any two, e.g. fasteners, seals, bindings.
   1.2) Award 1 mark each for any two, e.g. zips, press studs, velcro, buttons and poppers, decorative items.
   1.3) Award 1 mark each for any two, e.g. nuts and bolts, machine screws, rivets, hinges and washers.
   1.4) Award 1 mark each for any two, e.g. woodscrews, hinges, knock-down fittings.
2. Award marks as indicated, up to a maximum of 4 marks. For example: making components in small quantities can be very expensive [1] due to the labour time [1] and equipment required [1]. It normally costs less to buy standard components [1] and they can offer more consistent quality [1]. Any other relevant point.

## Page 187 Finishing Materials

1. 1 mark for each suitable finishing technique for each material. For example:

| Type of Material | Finishing Technique 1 | Finishing Technique 2 |
|---|---|---|
| Papers and boards | UV varnishing [1] | Embossing [1] |
| Timber-based materials | Varnishing [1] | Tanalising [1] |
| Metal-based materials | Dip-coating [1] | Galvanising [1] |
| Polymers | Polishing [1] | Vinyl decals [1] |
| Textile-based materials | Block printing [1] | Screen printing [1] |

2. 1 mark for the correct answer: c
3. It reduces the effects of friction [1].

## Page 188 Selection of Materials

1. 7–9 marks: thorough knowledge and understanding of the properties required, with a minimum of five properties considered. Explanations are given for why all the identified properties are needed. 4–6 marks: good knowledge and understanding of the properties required, with a minimum of three properties considered. Explanation included for why some of the identified properties are needed. 1–3 marks:

limited knowledge or understanding. Mainly descriptive response, stating a few of the properties required.

Properties specific to the application that could be considered include the following.

| Food packaging | • Absorbency, to prevent spoilage of contents or damage to the packaging<br>• Ability to be printed, to give aesthetic appeal<br>• Cost |
|---|---|
| Flat-pack furniture | • Toughness, to resist impacts<br>• Hardness, to resist being scratched or damaged in use<br>• Cost |
| Metal hammer | • Strength<br>• Toughness, to resist impact if hit or dropped<br>• Malleability, ability to be made into the shape of the tool (as material is very hard and may be difficult to form) |
| Plastic socket for an electric plug | • Electrical conductivity: it should be an insulator to protect the user from the electrical circuit inside it<br>• Toughness, so that it doesn't break if accidentally knocked, causing safety issues |
| Fabric covering for a sofa | • Aesthetics: colour and texture that appeal to the user<br>• Hardwearing so it lasts a long time<br>• Non-flammable, so that it does not burn |
| Electrical system in a fridge | • Absorbency and resistance to corrosion, so that it is not damaged by the materials, water or food that contact it in use<br>• Strength, to support whatever is put into it and to resist damage if someone sits on it!<br>• Electrical conductivity: it should insulate the circuitry to prevent electric shocks to the user |

In addition, general properties considered (in addition to the above list, where not duplicated) could include: functionality, aesthetics, environmental considerations, availability of materials, cost, social factors, ethical considerations and cultural factors.

## Page 189 Working with Materials

1. Award 1 mark each for up to four of the following: To achieve the properties needed in an application [1]. It costs less to reinforce just the area where enhanced properties are needed [1], rather than using a thicker material for the whole design [1] (which would also weigh more [1]) or a more expensive material with superior properties [1].
2. Award 1 mark for each suitable example and a further mark for correctly identifying the method of reinforcement. For example: battery holders [1] with webbing and internal ribs [1]; shirt collars [1] including interfacing [1]; disposable food trays [1] with bent (and sometimes folded) edges [1].

## Page 190 Scales of Manufacture

1. Award up to 10 marks as follows: one-off/bespoke production leads to the highest cost per product [1] as it requires the most labour time per product [1] and this labour is provided by highly skilled craftsmen [1]. Batch production groups identical products together which means that there is less non-making time due to equipment changeovers [1]. Dedicated jigs may be used to speed up production on some processes [1]. Some processes may be automated, speeding up production [1], as the cost can be divided between the quantity of products made [1]. Mass and continuous production lead to the lowest cost per product [1] when large

quantities of products are made [1]. Tools and equipment are dedicated to making one product [1], which means no time is lost to changing between products [1] and the high cost of the equipment can be divided between all of the products made [1]. Dedicated jigs and fixtures will be used [1] and most processes will be automated [1], speeding up production [1]. Labour costs are typically lower [1], as some lower-skill workers are used for production-line roles [1]. Any other relevant point.

## Page 191 Manufacturing Processes 1: Process Types and Processes used with Paper and Board

1. 1.1) Award up to 6 marks as follows: the sheet would need to be marked out [1], then cut using a rotary trimmer or guillotine [1]. The perforations for the tear-off tags [1] could be made using a perforation cutter [1]. The fold could be *either* manually scored [1], for example using scissors [1], and then folded *or* creased [1] with a creasing bar [1] then folded.
   1.2) Die cutting [1].

## Page 192 Manufacturing Processes 2: Timber-Based Materials

1. a) Any one of: coping saw, powered fretsaw, jigsaw and band saw [1]
   b) Smoothing plane [1]
   c) Bevel-edged chisel; also accept firmer chisel but not just 'chisel' [1]
   d) Sandpaper; also accept belt, disc or bobbin sander [1]
   e) Wood lathe [1]
   f) Rasp or surform; also accept gouge chisel [1]
2. Award up to 4 marks as follows (information can be in either sketches or notes): thin sheets of the timber [1] are glued together using PVA [1]. These are shaped round a former while the glue is wet [1] and clamped in place until the glue dries [1] when it will retain the shape of the former [1].

## Page 193 Manufacturing Processes 3: Metals and Alloys

1. Award marks as indicated up to a maximum of 6 marks: the parts to be joined are cleaned [1] and any oxide, rust or grease is removed [1]. They are placed together to form the joint [1]. A heat source from a flame/electric arc is applied [1]. This melts the edges of the parts so they join together [1]. A filler wire may be used [1] especially if there is a gap between the parts being joined [1]. The joint is then allowed to cool [1] and cleaned/descaled if necessary [1].
2. Award marks as indicated up to a maximum of 4 marks: brazing is carried out at a lower temperature than welding [1]. The parts to be joined do not melt [1]. A filler metal must be used; in welding this is sometimes not needed [1]. The joint is a different alloy to the parent metal [1]. A brazed joint is not normally as strong as a welded joint [1]. Any other relevant point.
3. Award 1 mark for either epoxy resin or riveting.

## Page 194 Manufacturing Processes 4: Polymers

1. Award marks as follows up to a maximum of 10 marks (information can be in either sketches or notes): a mould is made [1], the mould is placed inside the vacuum-forming machine [1], a sheet of material is clamped across the top [1], the material must be a thermoforming polymer [1], the material is heated until it softens [1], the mould is raised [1], a vacuum is applied to suck out the air between the mould and the plastic [1], air pressure from the atmosphere pushes the plastic against the mould [1], air may be blown in to help the mould release from the product [1], the mould is lowered and the plastic sheet is unclamped [1], the product is cut out of the plastic sheet [1].

### Page 195 Manufacturing Processes 5: Textiles and Electronic Systems

1. **1.1)** In pleating the folds are larger [1] and stitching may be at either the top or side [1].
   **1.2)** Award up to 5 marks as follows (information can be in either sketches or notes):
   wax is applied to the surface of the cloth [1], either by drawing the design with a spouted tool called a canting [1] or by printing with a copper stamp called a cap [1]. The cloth is then soaked in a dye [1]. Areas with the applied wax resist the dye and remain uncoloured [1]. The wax can then be removed with boiling water [1].
2. Solder paste is applied to a PCB [1] and the components positioned on their contact pads [1]. The whole assembly is then heated to melt the solder, creating the joint [1].

### Page 196 Measurement and Production Aids

1. Up to 2 marks for correct answer. For example: a reference point [1] on a material/product/object [1].
2. Up to 2 marks for explanation of each example. For example:
   - Jig: holding and positioning a drill [1] to ensure that holes are drilled in the same place on two pieces of wood [1].
   - Pattern: providing a pattern for a dress [1] so that the parts can be traced accurately onto fabric [1].

### Page 197 Ensuring Accuracy

1. Up to 2 marks for correct definition. For example: the degree of closeness of a measurement [1] to its true value/correct value/standard [1].
2. Up to 2 marks for explanation of each example. For example:
   - Quality control is about testing and checking [1] that a product meets the specification/a set of defined quality standards [1].
   - Quality assurance is putting systems in place [1] that ensure the quality of the processes used to manufacture the product [1].

### Page 198 Impact on Industry

1. Up to 2 marks each for explanation of advantage and disadvantage. For example:
   - Advantage: increased efficiency of manufacture [1] due to robots being able to work continuously [1].
   - Disadvantage: decreased employment opportunities [1] due to robots replacing people [1].
2. Up to 2 marks for definition. For example: a way for people to raise awareness and money for a project or idea [1], where people donate money in return for rewards [1].
3. 1 mark for suitable example. For example: email marketing to promote a product [1].

### Page 199 Impact on Production

1. Up to 2 marks for description. For example: lean manufacturing is an approach that aims to make products in the most effective and efficient way possible [1] by eliminating all forms of waste during manufacturing [1].
2. Up to 2 marks each for explanation of advantage and disadvantage. For example:
   - Advantage: less storage space is needed [1] because suppliers deliver materials only when they are required [1].
   - Disadvantage : production may have to be stopped [1] if materials are not delivered by suppliers on time [1].
3. Up to 2 marks for description of difference. For example: technology push is when new products are produced because of new materials/manufacturing methods becoming available [1], whereas market pull is when new products are developed because of market forces [1].
4. Any two of: laser cutter [1], vinyl cutter [1], 3D plotter [1], any other suitable CAM equipment [1].

### Page 200 Impact on Society and the Environment

1. 1 mark for each suitable improvement. For example: increase size of buttons [1], increase size of text on buttons/screen [1].
2. 1 mark for positive impact and 1 mark for negative impact. For example:
   - Positive impact: people can easily communicate with each other anytime/anywhere [1].
   - Negative impact: people can spend less time communicating face to face [1].
3. 1 mark for positive impact and 1 mark for negative impact. For example:
   - Positive impact: less pollution created from travelling [1].
   - Negative impact: increased electronic waste [1].

### Pages 202–207 Practice Exam Paper Section A

1. C [1]
2. A [1]
3. C [1]
4. D [1]
5. D [1]
6. A [1]
7. B [1]
8. D [1]
9. B [1]
10. A [1]
11. **11.1)** Award 1 mark for a suitable material. For example: shape memory alloy, thermochromic pigment or photochromic pigment.
    **11.2)** Award 1 mark for stating the property and 1 mark for stating the stimuli that it responds to. For example: shape memory alloy returns to its original shape [1] when heated [1]; thermochromic pigment changes colour [1] with temperature [1]; photochromic pigment changes colour/gets darker [1] with increasing brightness [1].
    **11.3)** Award 1 mark for stating a suitable application. For example: shape memory alloy: spectacle frames; thermochromic pigment: food packaging; photochromic pigment: sunglasses.
12. **12.1)** Output
    **12.2)** Input
13. 1 mark for each suitable disadvantage given. For example: more carbon emissions, will eventually run out.
14. 1 mark for each suitable advantage given. For example: less waste produced, reduced cost of buying new batteries.

### Pages 208–212 Practice Exam Paper Section B

15. A = 240 × sin 22° = 89.9 mm [1 mark for method, 1 mark for answer]
16. **16.1)** 1 mark for any suitable specific material. For example, polypropylene for outdoor seat. Material identified must be specific to gain a mark: plastic, wood, etc. should gain no marks.
    **16.2)** 3–4 marks: detailed response with at least two points explained further. 1–2 marks: one or two valid points presented but with little further explanation.
    For example: polypropylene is very strong [1] so could withstand applied forces without breaking [1]. Polypropylene is waterproof [1] so would not be damaged by rainfall [1].
    **16.3)** 1 mark for any suitable manufacturing process. For example: injection moulding for an outdoor seat.
    **16.4)** 1 mark for each suitable descriptive point up to a maximum of 5 marks. Points must be in the correct order for full marks. For example: injection moulding: plastic powder or granules are fed from a hopper into the machine [1]. Heaters melt the plastic as the screw moves it along towards the mould [1]. Once enough plastic has been melted, the screw forces the plastic into the mould [1]. Pressure is maintained on the mould [1] until it has cooled enough to be opened [1].

**17. 17.1)** Award 1 mark for nesting two shapes together to form a 400 × 300 mm rectangle; award a further mark for nesting the shapes as follows:

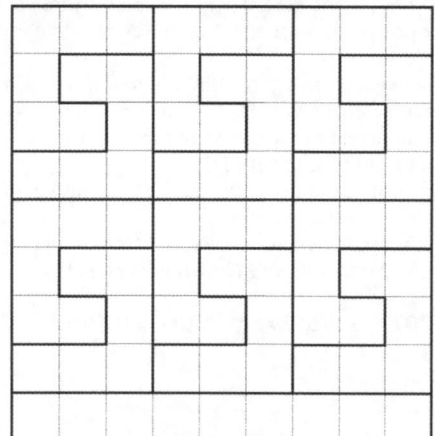

**17.2)** Area of one shape = 400 × 300 / 2 = 60,000 mm² (accept alternative methods) **[1]**

**17.3)** 1 mark for calculating the total area of the shapes (A). 1 mark for calculating the area of the sheet (B). 1 mark for calculating the amount of wasted material, C (B – A). 1 mark for calculating the percentage wasted = 1 – ((B – A) / B) × 100 / 1.
Calculations:
A = 12 × 60 000 = 720 000 mm² **[1]**
B = 900 × 900 = 810 000 mm² **[1]**
C = 810 000 – 720 000 = 90 000 mm² **[1]**
% = 90 000 / 810 000 × 100 / 1 = 11.1% **[1]**

**18.** 9–10 marks: balanced discussion that comes to a fully justified conclusion. All points discussed in detail. Excellent coverage. 7–8 marks: balanced discussion that comes to a conclusion, with some justification. Most points discussed in detail. Very good coverage. 5–6 marks: discussion with some balance. Some points discussed in detail. Good coverage. 3–4 marks: discussion lacks balance. Some points discussed, but may lack detail. Some coverage. 1–2 marks: mainly descriptive response with little discussion. Limited coverage.

Indicative answer: answer should discuss around the following points. For example: deforestation caused by use of timber-based materials: loss of habitats; drilling for oil for plastics/ mining for metal ore: impact on local ecosystem; farming for biomaterials: use of pesticides that can kill other animals; mileage of product throughout venture life cycle: cause of pollution; production of carbon from manufacturing products: impact on global warming.

## Pages 213–220 Practice Exam Paper Section C

**19. 19.1)** 1 mark for each suitable consideration. For example: aesthetics **[1]**, ergonomics **[1]**, function **[1]**, usability **[1]**.

**19.2)** For each factor: 3–4 marks: detailed evaluation with fully justified conclusions; 1–2 marks: limited evaluation. Some conclusions drawn but may not be justified.
For example: ergonomics: the headphones have padded ear muffs, which would make them comfortable to wear. The ear muffs are adjustable, so they can be moved to fit the correct size of head.

**20. 20.1)** 1 mark for each valid specification point and 1 mark for each supporting explanation. For example: the product must have images on the ear pieces **[1]** so it would be visually appealing to the child **[1]**. The product must have a fully adjustable headpiece **[1]** to accommodate the child growing **[1]**. The product must be simple to use **[1]** so it is accessible to the child **[1]**. The product must be made from durable materials **[1]** so it is not easily broken by the child **[1]**.

**20.2)** 1 mark for each designer and 1 mark for each explanation of influence. For example: Gerrit Rietveld **[1]**: use of only black, white and primary colours in the design **[1]**. Norman Foster **[1]**: use of latest technologies to improve the function of the product **[1]**.

**21. 21.1)** 1 mark for each valid descriptive point up to a maximum of 4 marks. A model is produced **[1]**. The model is tested/evaluated **[1]**. Changes/refinements are made **[1]**, leading to a new iteration **[1]**.

**21.2)** 5–6 marks: detailed, balanced discussion that comes to a fully justified conclusion. 3–4 marks: discussion with some detail but may focus overly on advantages or disadvantages. Comes to a conclusion but this may not be justified. 1–2 marks: mainly descriptive response. No conclusion.
Indicative answer: each iteration is fully tested and evaluated, so it is more likely that problems with the design will be discovered earlier. User feedback is constantly being gathered, which helps to ensure the design meets their needs. However, designers can become so focused on the current iteration that they sometimes lose sight of the bigger design picture. It can also be time consuming if a lot of prototypes or iterations need to be produced.

**22. 22.1)** 1 mark for each suitable point. For example: the permissible limits of variation **[1]** in the dimensions of a manufactured product **[1]**.

**22.2)** 1 mark for each suitable point up to a maximum of 4 marks. For example: so that manufacturers understand the importance of the dimensions/measurements that they have been given **[1]**. Failure to consider tolerances can lead to improper fits **[1]**, wasted materials **[1]** and the additional cost of remaking a product **[1]**.

**23. 23.1)** 20 **[1]**, 10% **[1]**

**23.2)** Award 1 mark for correct scaling. Award 1 mark for accurate drawing of the graph.

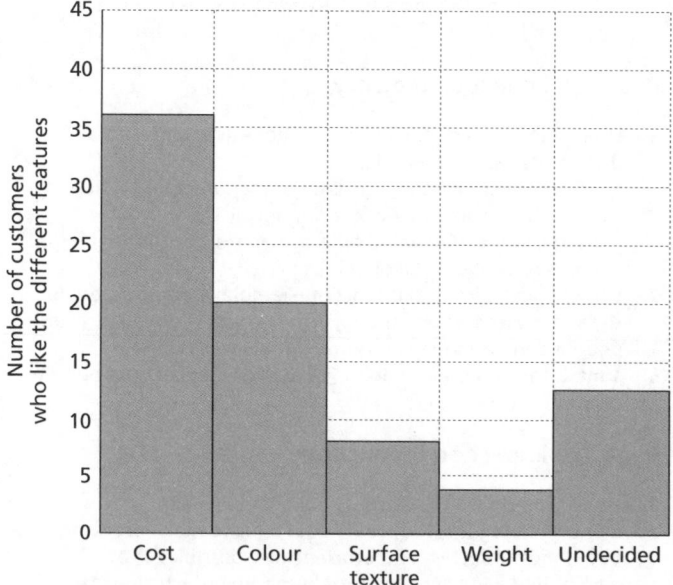

**23.3)** 1 mark for each type: primary **[1]**, secondary **[1]**.

# Notes

# Notes

# Notes

# Notes

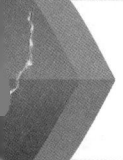

# Revision Tips

## Rethink Revision

Have you ever taken part in a quiz and thought '*I know this*!', but, despite frantically racking your brain, you just couldn't come up with the answer?

It's very frustrating when this happens, but in a fun situation it doesn't really matter. However, in your GCSE exams, it will be essential that you can recall the relevant information quickly when you need to.

Most students think that revision is about making sure you **know** stuff. Of course, this is important, but it is also about becoming confident that you can **retain** that *stuff* over time and **recall** it quickly when needed.

## Revision That Really Works

Experts have discovered that there are two techniques that help with all of these things and consistently produce better results in exams compared to other revision techniques.

Applying these techniques to your GCSE revision will ensure you get better results in your exams and will have all the relevant knowledge at your fingertips when you start studying for further qualifications, like AS and A Levels, or begin work.

It really isn't rocket science either – you simply need to:

- **test yourself** on each topic as many times as possible
- **leave a gap** between the test sessions.

It is most effective if you leave a good period of time between the test sessions, e.g. between a week and a month. The idea is that just as you start to forget the information, you force yourself to recall it again, keeping it fresh in your mind.

## Three Essential Revision Tips

1. **Use Your Time Wisely**
   - Allow yourself plenty of time.
   - Try to start revising six months before your exams – it's more effective and less stressful.
   - Your revision time is precious so use it wisely – using the techniques described on this page will ensure you revise effectively and efficiently and get the best results.
   - Don't waste time re-reading the same information over and over again – it's time-consuming and not effective!
2. **Make a Plan**
   - Identify all the topics you need to revise (this All-in-One Revision & Practice book will help you).
   - Plan at least five sessions for each topic.
   - One hour should be ample time to test yourself on the key ideas for a topic.
   - Spread out the practice sessions for each topic – the optimum time to leave between each session is about one month but, if this isn't possible, just make the gaps as big as realistically possible.
3. **Test Yourself**
   - Methods for testing yourself include: quizzes, practice questions, flashcards, past papers, explaining a topic to someone else, etc.
   - This All-in-One Revision & Practice book provides seven practice opportunities per topic.
   - Don't worry if you get an answer wrong – provided you check what the correct answer is, you are more likely to get the same or similar questions right in future!

Visit our website to download your free flashcards, for more information about the benefits of these revision techniques, and for further guidance on how to plan ahead and make them work for you.

# www.collins.co.uk/collinsGCSErevision

# Collins GCSE Revision

## ACKNOWLEDGEMENTS

The author and publisher are grateful to the copyright holders for permission to use quoted materials and imag

Cover, p.1, p.161 © violetblue/Shutterstock.com
p.14 © David Gee 1 / Alamy Stock Photo
p.93 © www.optitex.com
All other images © Shutterstock.com

Every effort has been made to trace copyright holde and obtain their permission for the use of copyright material. The author and publisher will gladly receive information enabling them to rectify any error or omission in subsequent editions. All facts are correct at time of going to press.

Published by Collins

An imprint of HarperCollins*Publishers* Ltd

1 London Bridge Street,
London, SE1 9GF

© HarperCollins*Publishers* Limited

9780008227401

First published 2017

10 9 8 7 6 5 4 3 2 1

British Library Cataloguing in Publication Data.

A CIP record of this book is available from the British Library.

Authored by: Paul Anderson and David Hills-Taylor
Project management and editorial: Nik Prowse
Commissioning: Katherine Wilkinson and Katie Gallowa
Cover Design: Sarah Duxbury and Paul Oates
Inside Concept Design: Sarah Duxbury and Paul Oat
Text Design and Layout: Jouve India Private Limited
Production: Natalia Rebow
Printed in the UK by Bell and Bain Ltd, Glasgow

## 6 EASY WAYS TO ORDER

1. Available from www.collins.co.uk
2. Fax your order to 01484 665736
3. Phone us on 0844 576 8126
4. Email us at education@harpercollins.co.
5. Post your order to: Collins Education, FREEPOST RTKB-SGZT-ZYJL, Honley HD9 6QZ
6. Or visit your local bookshop.

Visit the website to view the complete range and place an order:

# www.collins.co.uk/collinsGCSErevision